The Aquarian Sun Sign Guides

CAPRICORN

Bernard Fitzwalter has been interested in astrology since he was about six, when he played King Herod's astrologer in his primary school nativity play. For the past six years he has been teaching astrology for the Marylebone-Paddington Institute, and for seven years he has had a regular column in OVER 21 magazine. In 1984 he appeared in the first series of Anglia Television's *Zodiac Game*, which prompted the *Daily Mirror* to say that he was 'enough' to give astrology a good name'.

AQUARIAN SUN SIGN GUIDES

CAPRICORN

23 DECEMBER ~ 20 JANUARY

Bernard Fitzwalter

Cover illustration by Steinar Lund
Cover typography by Steven Lee

THE AQUARIAN PRESS
Wellingborough, Northamptonshire

First published 1987

British Library Cataloguing in Publication Data

Fitzwalter, Bernard
Capricorn.—(The Aquarian sun sign guides)
1. Zodiac
1. Title
133.5'4 BF1728.A2

ISBN 0-85030-578-0

The Aquarian Press is part of the Thorsons Publishing Group

Printed and bound in Great Britain

Contents

Introduction

This book has been written to help you find out a little about astrology and a lot about yourself. It explains, for the first time, the motives and aims that guide your actions and make you do things the way you do; what it does not do is give you a list of 'typical Capricorn' things to see if you recognize any of them. You are not likely to be typical anything: you are unique. What you *do* have in common with others who have birthdays at about the same time as you is a way of using your energy, a way of thinking, a set of motives and beliefs which seem to make sense to you, and which other people, those of the other eleven signs, obviously do not have. This book shows you those motives and beliefs, and shows you how they fit in with those of the other eleven signs. The zodiac is like a jigsaw: all the pieces have to be there for the whole picture to emerge.

This book also sets out to answer some very simple questions which are often asked but seldom answered. Questions like 'Why does the zodiac have twelve signs?' and 'What does being a Capricorn actually mean?' as well as 'Why are Capricorns supposed to be pessimistic? Why can't they be optimistic instead? and why don't all the people of the same star sign look the same?'

The reason that these questions are seldom answered is because all too many astrologers don't know the rudiments of astrological theory, and what they do know they don't tell, because they think it is too difficult for the man in the street to understand. This is obvious nonsense: astrology was devised for and by people who did not normally read or write as much as we do, nor did they all have PhDs or the equivalent. The man in the street is quite capable of understanding anything provided that it is shown simply and clearly, from first principles upwards, and provided he has sufficient interest. Buying this book is evidence enough of your interest, and I hope that the explanations are simple enough and clear enough for you. If they are not, it is my fault, and not that of astrology.

How to Use this Book

The book is in four parts. It is best to read them in sequence, but if you have neither time nor patience, then they each work individually. Part 2 does not assume that you have read Part 1, though it helps. Part 3 makes a lot more sense if you have already read Parts 1 and 2, but it isn't mandatory. Part 4, although just as firmly based on astrological principles as the other three, is deliberately intended as light relief to bring you back to real life gently after some of the more thought-provoking stuff.

The first part of the book deals with the theory behind the zodiac; it sets out the principles of astrology and enables you to see why Capricorn is assigned the qualities it has, how the ruling planet system works, and what all the other signs are like in terms of motivation, so you can compare them to your own. There is a short and effective method given for assessing the aims and motives of other people. When you read Part 3 you will need to know a bit about the other signs, as you will be finding out that you have more to you than just the Capricorn part you knew about.

The second part describes the essential Capricorn. It shows you how there are different sorts of Capricornians according to where your birthday falls in the month, and shows how Capricornian energy is used differently in the Capricorn as a child, adult, and parent.

Since you spend the greatest part of your life in dealing with other individuals, the way Capricorn deals with relationships is treated in some detail. This is the largest section of the book.

The third part shows you a different kind of zodiac, and enables you to go into your own life in much greater detail. It isn't complicated, but you do need to think. It crosses the border between the kind of astrology you get in the magazines, and the sort of thing a real astrologer does. There's no reason why you can't do it yourself because, after all, you know yourself best.

The fourth part shows you the surface of being a Capricorn, and how that zodiacal energy comes out in your clothes, your home, even your favourite food. The final item of this part actually explains the mechanics of being lucky, which you probably thought was impossible.

I hope that when you finish reading you will have a clearer view of yourself, and maybe like yourself a little more. Don't put the book away and forget about it; read it again in a few months' time—you will be surprised at what new thoughts about yourself it prompts you to form!

Note

Throughout this book, the pronouns 'he', 'him', and 'his' have been used to describe both male and female. Everything which applies to a male Capricorn applies to a female Capricorn as well. There are two reasons why I have not bothered to make the distinction: firstly, to avoid long-windedness; secondly, because astrologically there is no need. It is not possible to tell from a horoscope whether the person to whom it relates is male or female, because to astrology they are both living individuals full of potential.

BERNARD FITZWALTER

Part 1

How the Zodiac Works

1. The Meaning of the Zodiac

Two Times Two is Four; Four Times Three is Twelve

It is no accident that there are twelve signs in the zodiac, although there are a great many people who reckon themselves to be well versed in astrology who do not know the reasons why, and cannot remember ever having given thought to the principles behind the circle of twelve.

The theory is quite simple, and once you are familiar with it, it will enable you to see the motivation behind all the other signs as well as your own. What's more, you only have to learn nine words to do it. That's quite some trick—being able to understand what anybody else you will ever meet is trying to do, with nine words.

It works like this.

The zodiac is divided into twelve signs, as you know. Each of the twelve represents a stage in the life cycle of solar energy as it is embodied in the life of mankind here on our planet. There are tides in this energy; sometimes it flows one way, sometimes another, like the tides of the ocean. Sometimes it is held static, in the form of an object, and sometimes it is released when that object is broken down after a period of time. The twelve signs show all these processes, both physical and spiritual, in their interwoven pattern.

Six signs are used to show the flowing tide, so to speak, and six for the ebbing tide. Aries, Gemini, Leo, Libra, Sagittarius, and Aquarius are the 'flowing' group, and the others form the second group. You will notice at once that the signs alternate, one with the other, around the zodiac, so that the movement is maintained, and there is never a concentration of one sort of energy in one place. People whose Sun sign is in the first group tend to radiate their energies outwards from themselves. They are the ones who like to make the first move, like to be the ones to take command of a situation, like to put something of themselves into whatever they are doing. They don't feel right standing on the sidelines; they are the original have-a-go types. Energy comes out of them and is radiated towards other people, in the same way as the Sun's energy is radiated out to the rest of the solar system.

The people in the other signs are the opposite to that, as you would expect. They collect all the energy from the first group, keeping it for themselves and making sure none is wasted. They absorb things from a situation or from a personal contact, rather than contributing to it. They prefer to watch and learn rather than make the first move. They correspond to the Moon, which collects and reflects the energy of the Sun. One group puts energy out, one group takes it back in. The sum total of energy in the universe remains constant, and the two halves of the zodiac gently move to and fro with the tide of the energies.

This energy applies both to the real and concrete world of objects, as well as to the intangible world of thoughts inside our heads.

A distinction has to be made, then, between the real world and the intangible world. If this is done, we have four kinds of energy: outgoing and collecting, physical and mental. These four kinds of energy have been recognized for a long time, and were given names to describe the way they work more than two thousand years ago. These are the elements. All the energy in the cosmos can be described in the terms of these four: Fire, Earth, Air, Water.

Fire is used to describe that outgoing energy which applies to the real and physical world. There are three signs given to it: Aries, Leo, and Sagittarius. People with the Sun in any of these signs find themselves with the energy to get things going. They are at their best when making a personal contribution to a situation, and they expect to see some tangible results for their efforts. They are sensitive to the emotional content of anything, but that is not their prime concern, and so they tend to let it look after itself while they busy themselves with the actual matter in hand. Wherever you meet Fire energy in action, it will be shown as an individual whose personal warmth and enthusiasm are having a direct effect on his surroundings.

Earth is used to describe the real and physical world where the energies are being collected and stored, sometimes in the form of material or wealth. The three signs given to the element are Taurus, Virgo, and Capricorn. Where Fire energy in people makes them want to move things, Earth energy makes them want to hold things and stop them moving. The idea of touching and holding, and so that of possession, is important to these people, and you can usually see it at work in the way they behave towards their own possessions. The idea is to keep things stable, and to hold energy stored for some future time when it will be released. Earth Sun people work to ensure that wherever they are is secure and unlikely to change; if possible they would like the strength and wealth of their situation to increase, and will work towards that goal. Wherever you meet Earth energy in action, there will be more work being done than idle chat, and there will be a resistance to any kind of new idea. There will be money being made, and accumulated. The idea of putting down roots and bearing fruit may be a useful one to keep in mind when trying to understand the way this energy functions.

Air is used to describe outgoing mental energies; put more simply, this is communication. Here the ideas are formed in the mind of the individual, and put out in the hope that they can influence and meet the ideas of another individual; this is communication, in an abstract sense. Gemini, Libra, and Aquarius are all Air signs, and people with the Sun in those signs are very much concerned with communicating their energies to others. Whether anything gets done as a result of all the conversation is not actually important; if there is to be a concrete result, then that is the province of Fire or Earth energies. Here the emphasis is on shaping the concept, not the reality. There is an affinity with Fire energies, because both of them are outgoing, but other than that they do not cross over into each other's territory. Wherever you meet Air energy in action, there is a lot of talk, and new ideas are thrown up constantly, but there is no real or tangible result, no real product, and no emotional involvement; were there to be emotional content, the energies would be watery ones.

Water is the collection of mental energies. It is the response to communication or action. It absorbs and dissolves everything else, and puts nothing out. In a word, it is simply feelings. Everything emotional is watery by element, because it is a response to an outside stimulus and is often not communicated. It is not, at least not in its pure sense, active or initiatory, and it does not bring anything into being unless transformed into energy of a different type, such as Fire. Cancer, Scorpio and Pisces are the Water signs, and natives of those signs are often moody, withdrawn, and uncommunicative. Their energy collects the energy of others, and keeps their mental responses to external events stored. They are not being sad for any particular reason; it is simply the way that energy works. It is quite obvious that they are not showing an outgoing energy, but neither have they anything tangible to show for their efforts, like the money and property which seem to accumulate around Earth people. Water people simply absorb, keep to themselves, and do not communicate. To the onlooker, this appears unexciting, but there again the onlooker is biased: Fire and Air energies only appreciate outgoing energy forms, Earth energies recognize material rather than mental energies, and other Water energies are staying private and self-contained!

We now recognize four kinds of energy. Each of these comes in three distinct phases; if one zodiac sign is chosen to represent each of these phases within an element, there would be twelve different kinds of energy, and that would define the zodiac of twelve, with each one showing a distinct and different phase of the same endless flow of energy.

The first phase, not surprisingly, is a phase of definition, where the energies take that form for the first time, and where they are at their purest; they are not modified by time or circumstance, and what they aim to do is to start things in their own terms. These four most powerful signs (one for each element, remember) are called cardinal signs: Aries, Cancer, Libra, Capricorn. When the Sun enters any of these signs, the seasons change; the first day of the Sun's journey through Aries is the first day of spring, and the Spring equinox; Libra marks the Autumnal equinox, while Cancer and Capricorn mark Midsummer's Day and the shortest day respectively.

The second phase is where the energy is mature, and spreads itself a little; it is secure in its place, and the situation is well established, so there is a sort of thickening and settling of the energy flow. Here it is at its most immobile, even Air. The idea is one of maintenance and sustenance, keeping things going and keeping them strong. This stage is represented by Taurus, Leo, Scorpio, and Aquarius, and they are called, unsurprisingly, fixed signs. These four signs, and their symbols, are often taken to represent the four winds and the four directions North, South, East and West. Their symbols (with an eagle instead of a scorpion for Scorpio) turn up all over Europe as tokens for the evangelists Luke, Mark, John and Matthew (in that order).

The final phase is one of dissolution and change, as the energy finds itself applied to various purposes, and in doing so is changed into other forms. There is an emphasis on being used for the good, but being used up nonetheless. The final four signs are Gemini, Virgo, Sagittarius, and Pisces; in each of them the energies of their element are given back out for general use and benefit from where they had been maintained in the fixed phase. It is this idea of being used and changed which leads to this phase being called mutable.

Three phases of energy, then; one to form, one to grow strong and mature, and one to be used, and to become, at the end, something else. Like the waxing, full and waning phases of the Moon.

The diagram on page 16 shows the twelve signs arranged in

their sequence round the zodiac. Notice how cleverly the cycle and phases interweave:

(a) Outgoing and collecting energies alternate, with no two the same next to each other;

(b) Physical ebb and flow are followed by mental ebb and flow alternately in pairs round the circle, meaning that the elements follow in sequence round the circle three times;

(c) Cardinal, fixed, and mutable qualities follow in sequence round the circle four times, and yet

(d) No two elements or qualities the same are next to each other, even though their sequences are not broken.

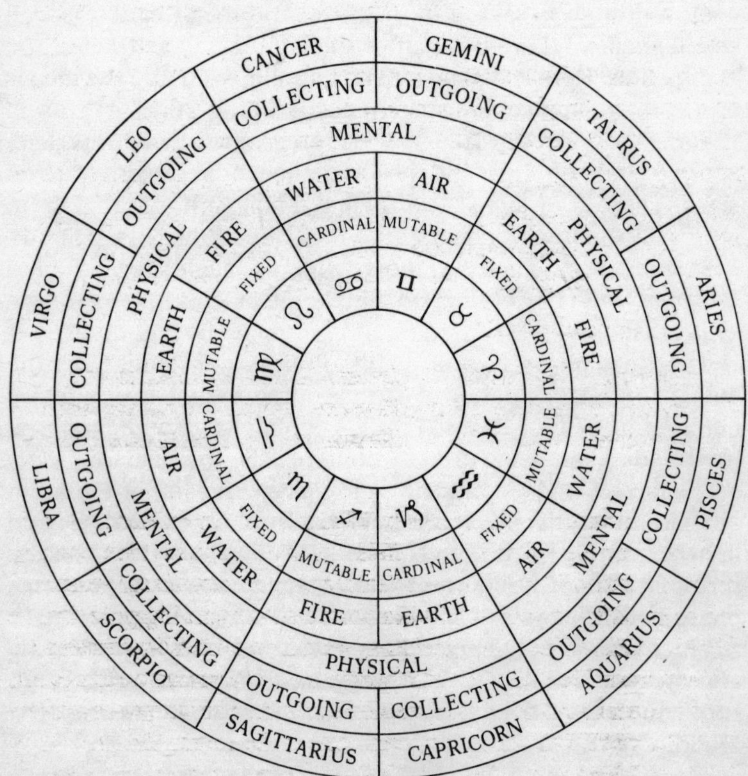

The interweaving is perfect. The zodiac shows all forms of energy, physical and mental, outgoing or incoming, waxing or waning, harmoniously forming a perfectly balanced unity when all the components are taken together. Humanity, as a whole, contains all the possibilities; each individual is a component necessary to the whole.

All this can be a bit long-winded when what you want is some way of holding all that information for instant recall and use, which is where the nine words come in.

If a single word is used for the kind of energy flow, and another two for the element and quality, then they can be used to form a sentence which will describe the way the energy is being used.

As a suggestion (use other words if they are more meaningful to you), try 'outgoing' and 'collecting' for the energy flows.

Next, for the elements:

Fire	:	activity	(Aries, Leo, Sagittarius)
Earth	:	material	(Taurus, Virgo, Capricorn)
Air	:	communication	(Gemini, Libra, Aquarius)
Water	:	feelings	(Cancer, Scorpio, Pisces)

And for the qualities:

Cardinal	:	defining	(Aries, Cancer, Libra, Capricorn)
Fixed	:	maintaining	(Taurus, Leo, Scorpio, Aquarius)
Mutable	:	using	(Gemini, Virgo, Sagittarius, Pisces)

Now in answer to the question 'What is a Gemini doing?' and answer can be formed as 'He's outgoing, and he's using communication', which neatly encapsulates the motivation of the sign. All that you need to know about the guiding principles of a Gemini individual, no matter who he is, is in that sentence. He will never deviate from that purpose, and you can adapt your own actions to partner or oppose his intention as you please.

A Scorpio? He's collecting, and he's maintaining his feelings. An Arian? He's outgoing, and he's defining activity. And so on.

Those nine words, or some similar ones which you like better, can be used to form effective and useful phrases which describe the motivation of everybody you will ever meet. How different people show it is their business, but their motivation and purpose is clear if you know their birthday.

Remember, too, that this motivation works at all levels, from the immediate to the eternal. The way a Taurean conducts himself in today's problems is a miniature of the way he is trying to achieve his medium-term ambitions over the next two or three years. It is also a miniature of his whole existence: when, as an old man, he looks back to see what he tried to do and what he achieved, both the efforts and the achievement, whatever it is, can be described in the same phrase with the same three words.

2.The Planets and the Horseshoe

You will have heard, or read, about the planets in an astrological context. You may have a horoscope in a magazine which says that Mars is here or Jupiter is there, and that as a consequence this or that is likely to happen to you. Two questions immediately spring to mind: What do the planets signify? How does that affect an individual?

The theory is straightforward again, and not as complex as that of the zodiac signs in the previous chapter. Remember that the basic theory of astrology is that since the universe and mankind are part of the same Creation, they both move in a similar fashion, so Man's movements mirror those of the heavens. So far, so good. If you look at the sky, night after night, or indeed day after day, it looks pretty much the same; the stars don't move much in relationship to each other, at least not enough to notice. What do move, though, are the Sun and Moon, and five other points of light—the planets. It must therefore follow that if these are the things which move, they must be the things which can be related to the movements of Man. Perhaps, the theory goes, they have areas of the sky in which they feel more at home, where the energy that they represent is stronger; there might be other places where they are uncomfortable and weak, corresponding to the times in your life when you just can't win no matter what you do. The planets would then behave like ludo counters, moving round the heavens trying to get back to a home of their own colour, and then starting a new game.

The scheme sounds plausible, makes a sort of common sense, and is endearingly human; all hallmarks of astrological thought, which unlike scientific thought has to relate everything to the human experience. And so it is: the planets are given values to show the universal energy in different forms, and given signs of the zodiac as homes. Therefore your Sun sign also has a planet to look after it, and the nature of that planet will show itself strongly in your character.

The planets used are the Sun and Moon, which aren't really planets at all, one being a satellite and the other a star, and then Mercury, Venus, Mars, Jupiter, and Saturn. This was enough until the eighteenth century, when Uranus was discovered, followed in the subsequent two hundred years by Neptune and Pluto. Some modern astrologers put the three new planets into horoscopes, but it really isn't necessary, and may not be such a good idea anyway. There are three good reasons for this:

(a) The modern planets break up the symmetry of the original system, which was perfectly harmonious;

(b) The old system is still good enough to describe everything that can happen in a human life, and the modern planets have little to add;

(c) Astrology is about the relationship between the sky and a human being. An ordinary human being cannot see the outer planets on his own; he needs a telescope. We should leave out of the system such things as are of an extra-human scale or magnitude: they do not apply to an ordinary human. If we put in things which are beyond ordinary human capabilities, we cannot relate them to the human experience, and we are wasting our time.

In the diagram on page 21, the zodiac is presented in its usual form, but it has also been split into two from the start of Leo to the start of Aquarius. The right hand half is called the solar half, and the other one is the lunar half. The Sun is assigned to Leo because in the Northern hemisphere, where astrology started, August is when you feel the influence of the Sun most, especially in the Eastern Mediterranean, where the Greeks and the other early Western civilizations were busy putting the framework of astrology together in the second millennium BC. The Sun is important because it gives light. The Moon gives light too; it is reflected sunlight, but it is enough to see by, and this is enough to give the Sun and Moon the title of 'the Lights' in astrology. The Moon is assigned to Cancer, so that the two of them can balance and complement each other. From there, moving away from the Lights around the circle on both sides, the signs have the planets assigned to them starting with the fastest mover, Mercury, and continuing in decreasing order of speed. Saturn is the slowest mover of all, and the two signs opposite to

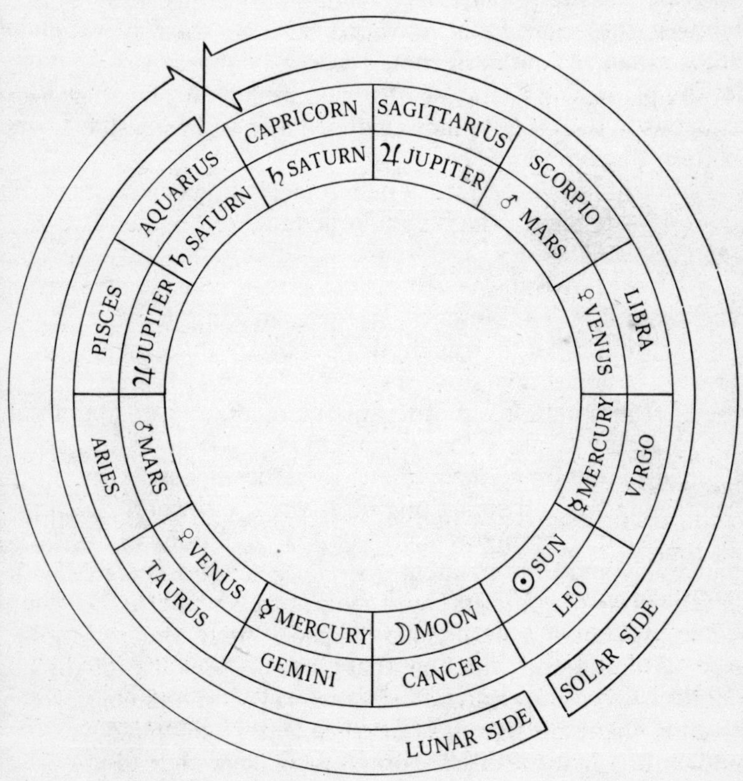

the Lights are both governed by that planet. The reasons for this apparent assymmetry will be explained in a little while. This arrangement is, of course, the horseshoe of the title to this chapter.

The Sun and Moon work in a similar fashion to the outgoing and collecting energies we noted earlier with the twelve signs. The Sun is radiant above all else; energy comes outwards from it, warming and energizing all those around it. Leo people, whose sign is the Sun's, work like this by being at the centre of a group of people and acting as inspiration and encouragement to them all. The Moon reflects the Sun's light, and energies of a lunar kind are directed inwards towards the core of the person. The two energies are necessarily linked; lunar people would starve without the solar folks' warmth, but the solar types need someone to radiate to or their purpose is unfulfilled.

The planets on each side of the horseshoe display their own energies in a solar or lunar way depending on which side of the pattern they are on.

Mercury and Venus form a pair, representing complementary but opposite ideas, which should be familiar by now. Mercury represents difference, and Venus stands for similarity.

Wherever anything new forms that is distinguishable from the background, then Mercury is there making it what it is, highlighting what makes it different. Anything separate is Mercurial, and words, since they are separate and can be strung together into millions of different combinations, are Mercurial too. Mercury is not a long-term influence; it notes things as being different for an instant, and then they become part of the establishment, and something else is new elsewhere. Because 'new' is an instantaneous state—that is, something can only be new once, and for a moment—Mercury is not associated with anything lasting, and its rapid motion as a planet leads to its being associated with the idea of speed. Virgo, Mercury's solar sign, is concerned with the changing of the shape of things ('collecting, using material' in our keyword system), while Gemini, the lunar sign, is concerned with reading and writing, and getting new ideas ('outgoing, using communication').

Venus does the reverse; it looks for that which is similar, finding points of contact to make relationships between common interests and energies. It likes to preserve the harmonies of life, and resents anything which might interrupt them. Love and affection are naturally Venusian, but so is music and all of the Arts, for the harmonies they contain. Expressed in a solar way, Venus is Libra, the maker of relationships; its lunar face is Taurus, emphasizing food and furnishings as things which give pleasure to the individual.

The next pair are Mars and Jupiter. Mars applies force from the outside to impose structure on a disordered universe, while Jupiter expands forcibly from the inside to give growth and wealth, inviting everyone else to join in.

Mars is pure force, energy in a straight line with a direction to go in. Anger and passion are both Martian, and so is lust, because they are all examples of great energy directed towards a given end. Note that Martian force is not necessarily strength, wealth, or know-how, just pure energy, which often boils over and needs controlling. Mars is the power in an athlete, and in an assassin too. It is also the power in a lover, because the urge to create is also the urge to pro-create, and if that energy fulfils its purpose then that creation takes place. Scorpio is its solar side, the power to control and create; in lunar form it is shown by Aries, as energy enjoyed for its own sake by its owner, with no purpose except to express it.

Jupiter is the spirit of expansion from within; not only does it oppose Mars' force from outside, it opposes Mars' physicality with its own mental emphasis. Jupiter develops the mind, then. As it does so, it develops all natural talents of an academic nature, and encourages movement, enquiry and travel to broaden experience and knowledge. The Solar expression of this is Sagittarius, where the centaur symbol is both a wise teacher and a free-roaming wild horse at the same time. Jupiter in a lunar sense is Pisces, where the imagination is developed to a greater extent than anywhere else, but used to provide an internal dream world for the owner's pleasure. Great sensitivity here, but the lunar energies are not of the sort to be expressed; rather other energies are *im*pressed on the Piscean mind.

Saturn is the last of the five planets. He stands alone, and if it is necessary to consider him as paired with anything it is with the Lights as an entity together. The Lights are at the centre of the system; Saturn is at its edge. They are the originators of the energies of the zodiac, and he is the terminator. Everything to do with limits and ends is his. He represents Time, and lots of it, in contrast to Mercury, which represented the instant. He represents the sum total of all things, and the great structures and frameworks of long-term endeavour. In solar form he is Capricorn, the representative of hard work, all hierarchies, and all rulers; in lunar form he is Aquarius, showing the horizontal structure of groups of people within society at different levels. Here he denies the activity of Mars, because society is too big for one person to change against the collective will, and he contains the expansion of Jupiter within himself. Venus and Mercury can neither relate to it nor make it change, because it is always the same, in the end.

The planets show important principles in action, the same as the zodiac does. You have probably noticed that the horseshoe of the planets and the ring of the zodiac say the same thing in a different way, and that is true about most things in astrology. It may be that the two systems interrelate and overlap because they are from the same source: after all, 3+2+2=7, which is the planet's total, and 3x2x2=12, which is the signs'. How you assign the elements and qualities, pairs of planets and lights is for you to decide. The joy of astrology, like all magic, is that it has you at the centre, and is made to fit its user's requirements. Now you know the principles, you can use it as you please, and as it seems relevant to you.

Part 2

Yourself—and Others

3. The Essential Capricorn

All the energy in the zodiac is solar, but that solar energy takes many forms. It is moderated and distributed through the planetary energies until it finally shows in you, the individual. As a Capricorn, the prime planetary energy is that of Saturn; you will be motivated by, and behave in the manner of, the energies of Saturn. To remind yourself of what that means, read the section on Saturn on page 24. As a sign of the zodiac, Capricorn is a Cardinal Earth sign. Remind yourself what that means by reading page 17. Now we have to see how those essential principles work when expressed through a person and his motivation.

What it Means to be a Capricorn

You know what it is to be a Capricorn, because you are one; but you probably don't know what it is that makes a Capricorn the way he is, because you cannot stand outside yourself. You would have to be each of the other eleven signs in turn to understand the nature of the energy that motivates you. This essential energy is in every Capricorn, but it shows itself to different extents and in different ways. Because it is in every single Capricorn, it is universal rather than specific, and universal ideas tend to come in language which sounds a little on the woolly side. You will think that it isn't really about what makes you who you are, because you don't feel like that every day—or at least you think you don't. In fact, you feel like that all the time, but you don't notice it any more than you notice your eyes focusing, yet they do it all the time, and you see things the way you do because of it.

The first thing to note is that the zodiac is a circle, not a line with a beginning and an end. If it were a line, then Capricorn would be three-quarters of the way along it, but that would be to miss the point; if the zodiac is a circle, then Capricorn is a stage in an endlessly repeating cycle, and we will get a much better idea of what it is if we look to see where it came from, and where it is going.

The sign before Capricorn is Sagittarius. Sagittarius represents that stage where being sure of yourself produces the confidence to give yourself to others without fear of losing anything. It is similar to the process of teaching, where information and skill is passed on to a wider group for the good of the group rather than the good of the teacher. It is to do with putting ideas out to a wider audience. When those ideas are put into action, and made to produce results, then that is no longer Sagittarius. When the teacher's reputation increases, and he is recognized as a person of importance because of what he knows, that is not Sagittarius either. When a group of ideas become fixed into a set way of doing things, a routine if you like, then they are no longer Sagittarian. Whenever knowledge or ideas are changed into visible results, Sagittarius becomes Capricorn.

The ideas of Sagittarius become the achievemens of Capricorn. The outward energy of the Fire sign idea becomes collected and set in the form of the Earth sign object. Capricorn energy is nearly always in the form a visible object; it tries to encapsulate all the time, effort, ideas, money, planning, dedication, and heartache that went into something by having a visible object by which the achievement is measured. Capricorn people buy themselves big cars and big houses as a reward to themselves for their achievements; they say 'I wanted to have something to show for it all'. How right they are: Capricorn must not only have visible results, but it likes to show them off, and it likes to be admired, too. The recognition and the reputation that goes with it are absolutely vital to Capricorn thought: if it doesn't add to your reputation, it isn't worth doing.

It sounds rather selfish, and it is, though to be fair it is actually self-centred, which is a different thing. All of the collecting signs are self-centred, but only two of them (Cancer and Capricorn) are cardinal as well, so only these two are so noticeable in the way that they look after themselves first. Eventually the wealth and achievement of Capricorn is shared with others, and used for good causes in an attempt to improve the chances of those less fortunate. To use the wealth of the individual for the good of society is the activity of the next sign in the cycle, Aquarius, which takes us further round the zodiac than we want to go for the moment; let's return to Capricorn.

Capricorn's ruling planet is Saturn, as we have already noted. Saturn is the last planet of the traditional 'seven stars'; after all the growth and change that the energies of the other six have made possible, Saturn puts the lid on, and gives things their final form. He is the planet of frameworks and containers; he is the much-quoted 'bottom line' of long and involved contracts. When all the fancy words and promises have evaporated, the reality of the affair is Saturn. The hard work necessary to keep things going is Saturn. The rules and regulations necessary to stop the whole thing falling apart are Saturn. Hard work, duty, being serious, getting results, being disciplined, keeping to the rules, putting in the hours necessary: all of these are the energies of Saturn, and it is these that the Capricorn is concerned with. Not that it is all bad: hard work and patience usually bring promotion, doing your duty usually gets you a medal, you are usually paid for putting in the hours; all of these are visible rewards, and as such appreciated by a Capricorn. Saturn is lord of structure and time; he puts things in their places, and keeps them there for ever. A Capricorn person, with Saturn's energies in him, enjoys finding things in their places, and keeping to his. He has enormous stamina, because Saturn will give him both strength and time together. He is not as explosively powerful as Mars' people, or as creative as Jupiter's, but he can maintain his efforts over a long period, which other planets' people cannot.

Perhaps the greatest advantage a Capricorn has is his facility for turning time and energy into money, and from there into tokens of success, such as big cars and houses. 'Advantage' and 'facility' are perhaps the wrong words—a Capricorn can do nothing else *except* turn time and energy into money, but it is a feature of our society that we treat such a thing as being desirable, and define success as being that very process.

Capricorns, then, are the successes of society; when we think of material wealth and achievement, we are thinking in a Capricornian way, and all our status symbols are products of Capricorn thought. Each sign contributes its role to society—Arians provide the initial impetus, Virgoans the crafts and skills; Capricorns are the workers, the builders, the achievers.

Seeing the Capricorn in that way, like an organ in the body of the nation, leads to an interesting thought: if astrology maintains, as it does, that things exist in the same way at different levels, then is here a Capricornian organ in the body which functions in the same way for the individual as the Capricorn himself functions for society? The answer is yes, though in the case of Capricorn the parts of the body are not strictly organs. They are your bones and your skin.

Bones and skin are wonderful symbols for how a Capricorn thinks and works; one is the framework on which your body is built, and the other is what people actually see of you. Compare that to the Capricorn's liking for structures and rules, so that he knows where he is and what he has to do. Compare also the structure of bone, dry and hard, to the no-nonsense, serious, and sometimes rather pessimistic view of life that the Capricorn displays (not to mention his sense of humour, which is very dry indeed). Compare the function of skin as an outer covering to the Capricorn's desire for his achievements to be recognized, and his love of status symbols. Saturn, of course, represents both parts of the body at once. It is the outer envelope of the seven-planet solar system, as the skin is the outer envelope of the body, and it is the planet which gives structure, as the skeleton does. There are all sorts of phrases in everyday use which show how people have recognized Saturn and Capricorn over the years—'all skin and bone' suggests an animal which has had a hard time, and 'having old bones' is used by somebody who realizes his age. You can probably think of a few more.

The essence of the Capricorn, then, is about defining the structure of things, and working hard within the rules to achieve, and be recognized for, material success. Organized structure and reputation—bones and skin.

If the idea of bones and skin doesn't appeal as an image for your activities, then look to the animal symbol of your sign. Capricorn goats are tough and hardy beasts, with endless stamina. They keep on going, and they don't eat much—unlike sheep, who are much less determined and ambitious, and will opt for an easier life if they can. What goats really want is to get to the top of the mountain, to stand alone on the highest point of all, so that everyone else can see that they have made it to the top.

The Capricorn goat in the sky is actually two animals in one—he has the tail of a fish. Anything aquatic in astrology is a reference to spiritual and emotional values. In this case, because Capricorn is so practical, the message is not about ethereal or philosophical values, but about the wisdom of experience which Capricorns build up over a period of time. Capricorn doesn't just chase money and a bigger house—he acquires them on the way, but all the time he is thinking about the structure of things, appreciating the reasons why things are the way they are. A Capricorn is conventional, sure, but not from lack of thought; he wants things to continue as they are because in his opinion it would be better for everyone if they did. That's part of why the goat has a fish's tail.

Early, Middle or Late? The Decanates

Each of the zodiac signs is divided into degrees, like an arc of any other circle. Since a circle has 360 degrees, then each sign must be 30 degrees, since there are twelve signs. Each of the signs is further split into sections of ten degrees, called decanates. There are three decanates in each sign, and the one that your birthday falls in will tell you a little more about how that Capricorn energy actually works in you as an individual.

First decanate (22–31December)

This is the purest form of Capricorn. There is a double helping of Saturnine energy here, expressed as an appreciation of all hierarchies. To you, chains of control and command are good and necessary things, a belief which you will have considerable trouble explaining to any Sagittarian or Aquarian. To you, a pyramidal power of structure, with the boss at the top, then the managers and executives, and the juniors at the bottom, is the natural way of things. You feel at home in such a system, and you can use its rigid structure as a ladder to help your own progress upwards; each step is clearly defined, and unlikely to move under your feet.

The government of a country, not surprisingly, is assigned to this part of Capricorn; perhaps you will find yourself attracted to government as a career. There are lots of Capricornian politicians, and even if you don't want to be in the public eye there are thousands of Capricornian civil servants and local government officers, all of whom appreciate the firm and definite structure of their respective organizations. The same goes for banks, and in fact virtually any large corporate structure: they are all Capricornian if they have a defined hierarchy, and if you are from this sector of the sign you will be able to identify with that.

There are family hierarchies, too: this part of Capricorn is concerned with your parents, and you will probably find that a large part of your life is taken up with your duty to them. Perhaps you go into your father's business, or take up a trade which he would like to see you in. Perhaps you are dependent on his position and wealth for your own.

The business of Capricorn is to work to improve your position and reputation; in this decanate the position matters to you more than the reputation.

Second decanate (1–10 January)

The second decanate sees the influence of Saturn softened by that of Venus. The appreciation of structure and material is still there, of course, but the emphasis on hierarchy and your position within it has gone. What you are concerned with is the rewards for your effort. All forms of recognition for effort are in this part of the sign. Public honours are here, like knighthoods and MBEs, and so are status symbols, like black BMWs and Porsches. That doesn't mean that in every case if your birthday is here that you will be knighted, but it does mean that such things are important to you, and most of your energy is directed towards gaining some kind of public recognition for your efforts.

You are not the sort of person who wants to struggle through life, gamely plodding on doing something for duty's sake and not enjoying a single moment of it. You're not afraid of hard work, but you want to work hard at something you like, and to be handsomely rewarded for it. You would like to work hard at enjoying your rewards, too, and be appreciated for what you've attained in life. There's no virtue in having power and money if you don't use it, according to you, and there's certainly no use in having a limousine in your garage if you don't take it out and drive it now and again. You're not the sort to apologise for taking a limousine to the supermarket: you want to enjoy your car, and you want to enjoy people noticing that you've got one.

This is the decanate of the self-made man, who gets to the top through pure hard work, and enjoys being there. The goal is not the position itself, because hierarchies don't interest you; what matters is the prestige, the public recognition.

Third decanate (11–19 January)

In the final decanate the power of Saturn is mixed with Mercury's influence. In this section the position and the recognition are simply distant goals; what matters is the work itself. Mercury always deals on a small scale: with Saturn to keep its nose to the grindstone, so to speak, the result is a concentration on working, working in an effective, controlled, and practical way.

Saturn and Mercury together are the signature of rational thought; if your birthday is here you probably have a very cool and rational way of looking at things. You won't think of yourself or your preferences, just of the job that has to be done, and how it should be approached. The effect is one of logical practicality and disciplined application—imagination and originality are nowhere to be seen in this sort of process, and neither is any personal or emotional bias. It's not a cold way of thinking, as in ruthless and cruel, but it is a dry one, as in unfeeling and inflexible.

If Capricorn is to be able to turn ideas into objects, which is its purpose, then the way it works is important. This is the part of the sign which cares about the actual way things get done. Rules and regulations are given to this part of the sign, including Acts of Parliament and other such ways in which the Government, as a Capricornian institution, performs its function. If your birthday is here, the way things get done is more important to you than what you are doing them for; that things are done properly and effectively, in accordance with the rules, is often more important than anything else. What you can't stand is people who cut corners in their rush to get things finished, and people who want the glory of achievement without necessarily doing all of the work—as often occurs with people from the other two decanates, in fact.

Three Phases of Life: Capricorn as Child, Adult, Parent

The Capricorn Child

Capricorn children are apt to be quiet and careful. When very young, they make sure that they are not in any sort of a danger: they look at things like high trees and rivers and think about them rather than fall out of them or into them as other children do. Saturn gives a naturally cautious approach and a strong sense of self-preservation, and as a consequence Capricorn children manage to avoid the physical accidents which seem to feature in the lives of, for example, Fire-sign children.

At school, they are never very creative, nor expressive; they much prefer learning about things which have no element of personal expression in them, such as mathematics and science. Poetry and art, or any other activities where imagination and self-expression are called for, become something which the Capricorn child hopes to get through with as little fuss as possible, preferably without being asked to contribute something in front of the whole class. The reasons for this are simply that such activities are unstructured, and the Capricorn child is much better at following the rules than relying on his own creativity.

He will react very positively to praise from an early age. It is as though he doesn't know how good he is until somebody tells him, and the procedure of hard work followed by recognition of his efforts is one which he will continue to enjoy for the rest of his life.

Capricorn children are often given positions of responsibility at school, such as being made prefect or something like that. Because there is something of the old man in every Capricorn (Saturn showing itself again), they often seem mature and reliable to their teachers, and this may help them to win such promotions, but there is more to it than that. What actually takes place is that the Capricorn child quickly identifies the command structure within the school, and learns, too, what sort of behaviour is appropriate for progress up through that structure. It is an instinctive thing, in the same way that a vine will climb a trellis.

The Capricorn Adult

Climbing the trellis is the essential activity of the Capricorn adult's life, too. Capricorns and big organizations were made for each other. The Capricorn shows that he recognizes the importance of the organization by seeking to climb it, and the organization shows its recognition of his efforts by rewarding him with promotion. The organization sees no harm in this: after all, it is trying to maintain itself, and to take on board people who sincerely believe in the system itself must be good for the system. The organization knows that as the Capricorn rises through the hierarchy he will do all that he can to maintain and care for the system beneath him, because it is that which gives him his position; both sides benefit from this, and everything works very well.

An adult Capricorn will try to avoid anything that is new, untried, irregular, unconventional, or just plain revolutionary, and it is not because he fears for his safety; no, he learned how to avoid physical risks as an infant, and he doesn't have to think about it now. What he fears is the loss of his position. Anything which undermines the system brings with it various side-effects which the Capricorn would rather avoid. It could be that somebody takes a shortcut to the top; this would suggest either that the existing hierarchy is irrelevant, or that hard work isn't necessarily the best route to the top—both very upsetting ideas from a Capricornian view. At the very least, it suggests that the intruder is out of his proper place, acting above his station—another un-Saturnine idea. Then again, it might be that revolutionary changes might sweep away all the people who are in an inferior position to the Capricorn, which brings him down to ground level again, and removes the prestige attached to his progress so far. Again, such things are un-Capricornian.

The older he gets, and the further up the ladder, the less adventurous and more conservative the Capricorn becomes; he has more to lose than he could possibly gain by being innovative, so he stays with the structure as it is. What he wants, at the end of his day, is to have finished with more than he started with, and for his achievements to be recognized. The Capricorn's ultimate achievement is to build something which will have his name on it for all to see, and which will continue to embody his achievement long after he has gone.

The Capricorn Parent

Capricorn parents work hard for their children's benefit, but they expect their children to work hard for them in return. To the Capricorn parent, the child is the next stage down in the family hierarchy; those qualities which the parent admired in his parent are to be instilled into the child, so that the family continues in the traditions of achievement and excellence. The parent also expects the child to recognize the achievements of the parent, and to be suitably respectful; alas, children are seldom interested in traditions of excellence, and must usually reach the age of the parent themselves before they realize what it was that their parents wanted them to do.

The thing that children usually seem to bring out in a Capricorn parent is inflexibility. Capricorns think along fairly traditional lines, and by the time they are parents are usually quite set in their opinions; children think differently, and much more quickly, which shows the parent as inflexible by comparison.

Capricorn parents will make sure that their children have a better standard of material wealth than they themselves had. Partly this is because if they didn't, it would seem as though the family was making no progress over the generations, and partly it is because the parents want admiration for their children too, and the best way they know to do that is through status symbols. They don't always give their children as much pure affection as they might, which is one of the failings of the sign; any kind of energy, emotional included, gets transformed into material wealth by a Capricorn sooner or later. Saturn isn't a warm planet anyway, so its people can't be as demonstrative or as intimate as the other signs even if they try.

4. Capricorn Relationships

How Zodiacal Relationships Work

You might think that relationships between two people, described in terms of their zodiac signs, might come in 144 varieties; that is, twelve possible partners for each of the twelve signs. The whole business is a lot simpler than that. There are only seven varieties of relationship, although each of those has two people in it, of course, and the role you play depends on which end of the relationship you are at.

You may well have read before about how you are supposed to be suited to one particular sign or another. The truth is usually different. Capricorns are supposed to get on with Taureans and Virgoans, and indeed they do, for the most part, but it is no use reading that if you have always found yourself attracted to Leos, is it? There has to be a reason why you keep finding Leos attractive, and it is not always to do with your Sun sign; other factors in your horoscope will have a lot to do with it. The reason you prefer people of certain signs as friends or partners is because the relationship of your sign to theirs produces the sort of qualities you are looking for, the sort of behaviour you find satisfactory. When you have identified which of the seven types of basic relationship it is, you can see which signs will produce that along with your own, and then read the motivation behind it explained later on in more detail in 'The Capricorn Approach to

Relationships' and the individual compatibility sections.

Look at the diagram on page 16. All you have to do is see how far away from you round the zodiacal circle your partner's Sun sign is. If they are Gemini, they are five signs in front of you. You are also, of course, five signs behind them, which is also important, as you will see in a little while. If they are Libra, they are three signs behind you, and you are three signs in front of them. There are seven possibilities: you can be anything up to six signs apart, or you can both be of the same sign.

Here are the patterns of behaviour for the seven relationship types.

Same sign

Somebody who is of the same sign as you acts in the same way that you do, and is trying to achieve the same result for himself. If your goals permit two winners, this is fine, but if only one of you can be on top, you will argue. No matter how temperamental, stubborn, devious, or critical you can be, they can be just the same, and it may not be possible for you to take the same kind of punishment you hand out to others. In addition, they will display every quality which really annoys you about yourself, so that you are constantly reminded of it in yourself as well as in them. Essentially, you are fighting for the same space, and the amount of tolerance you have is the determining factor in the survival of this relationship.

One sign apart

Someone one sign forward from you acts as an environment for you to grow in. In time, you will take on those qualities yourself. When you have new ideas, they can often provide the encouragement to put them into practice, and seem to have all your requirements easily available. Often, it is this feeling that they already know all the pitfalls that you are struggling over which can be annoying; they always seem to be one step ahead of you, and can seemingly do without effort all the things which you have to sweat to achieve. If the relationship works well, they are helpful to you, but there can be bitterness and jealousy if it doesn't.

Someone one sign back from you can act as a retreat from the pressures of the world. They seem to understand your particular needs for rest and recovery, whatever they may be, and can usually provide them. They can hold and understand your innermost secrets and fears; indeed, their mind works best with the things you fear most, and the fact that they can handle these so easily is a great help to you. If the relationship is going through a bad patch, their role as controller of your fears gets worrying, and you will feel unnerved in their presence, as though they were in control of you. When things are good, you feel secure with them behind you.

Two signs apart
Someone two signs forward from you acts like a brother or sister. They are great friends, and you feel equals in each other's company; there is no hint of the parent-child or master-servant relationship. They encourage you to talk, even if you are reticent in most other company; the most frequently heard description of these relationships is 'We make each other laugh'. Such a partner can always help you put into words the things that you want to say, and is there to help you say them. This is the relationship that teenagers enjoy with their 'best friend'. There is love, but it does not usually take sexual form, because both partners know that it would spoil the relationship by adding an element of unnecessary depth and weight.

Someone two signs behind you is a good friend and companion, but not as intimate as somebody two signs forward. They are the sort of people you love to meet socially; they are reliable and honest, but not so close that things become suffocatingly intense. They stop you getting too serious about life, and turn your thoughts outwards instead of inwards, involving you with other people. They stop you from being too selfish, and help you give the best of yourself to others. This relationship, then, has a cool end and a warm end; the leading sign feels much closer to his partner than the trailing sign does, but they are both satisfied by the relationship. They particularly value its chatty quality, the fact that it works even better when in a group, and its tone of affection and endearment rather than passion and obsession.

Three signs apart

Someone three signs in front of you represents a challenge of some kind or another. The energies of the pair of you can never run parallel, and so must meet at some time or another. Not head on, but across each other, and out of this you can both make something strong and well established which will serve the two of you as a firm base for the future. You will be surprised to find how fiercely this person will fight on your behalf, or for your protection; you may not think you need it, and you will be surprised that anybody would think of doing it, but it is so nonetheless.

Someone three signs behind you is also a challenge, and for the same reasons as stated above; from this end of the relationship, though, they will help you achieve the very best you are capable of in a material sense. They will see to it that you receive all the credit that is due to you for your efforts, and that everyone thinks well of you. Your reputation is their business, and they will do things with it that you could never manage yourself. It's like having your own P.R. team. This relationship works hard, gets results, and makes sure the world knows it. It also looks after itself, but it needs a lot of effort putting in.

Four signs apart

Someone four signs forward from you is the expression of yourself. All the things you wanted to be, however daring, witty, sexy, or whatever, they already are, and you can watch them doing it. They can also help you to be these things. They do things which you think are risky, and seem to get away with them. There are things you aim towards, sometimes a way of life that you would like to have, which these people seem to be able to live all the time; it doesn't seem to worry them that things might go wrong. There are lots of things in their life which frighten you, which you would lie awake at nights worrying about, which they accept with a child's trust, and which never go wrong for them. You wish you could be like that.

Someone four signs behind you is an inspiration to you. All the things you wish you knew, they know already. They seem so wise and experienced, and you feel such an amateur; luckily, they are kind and caring teachers. They are convincing, too. When they speak, you listen and believe. It's nice to know there's somebody there with all the answers. This extraordinary relationship often functions as a mutual admiration society, with each end wishing it could be more like the other; unfortunately, it is far less productive than the three-sign separation, and much of its promise remains unfulfilled. Laziness is one of the inherent qualities of a four-sign separation; all its energies are fulfilled, and it rarely looks outside itself for something to act upon. Perhaps this is just as well for the rest of us.

Five signs apart

Someone five signs ahead of you is your technique. You know what you want to do; this person knows how to do it. He can find ways and means for you to do what you want to be involved in, and he can watch you while you learn and correct your mistakes. They know the right way to go about things, and have the clarity of thought and analytical approach necessary if you are to get things clear in your mind before you get started

Someone five signs behind you is your resource. Whenever you run out of impetus or energy, they step forward and support you. When you're broke, they lend you money, and seldom want it returned. When you need a steadying hand because you think you've over-reached yourself, they provide it. All this they do because they know that it's in their best interest as well as yours, to help you do things, and to provide the material for you to work with. You can always rely on them for help, and it's nice to know they will always be there. They cannot use all their talent on their own; they need you to show them how it should be done. Between you, you will use all that you both have to offer effectively and fully, but it is a relationship of cooperation and giving; not all the zodiac signs can make it work well enough.

Six signs apart

Someone six signs apart from you, either forwards or backwards, is both opponent and partner at the same time. You are both essentially concerned with the same area of life, and have the same priorities. Yet you both approach your common interests from opposite directions, and hope to use them in opposite ways. Where one is private, the other is public, and where one is self-centred, the other shares himself cheerfully. The failings in your own make-up are complemented by the strengths in the other; it is as if, between you, you make one whole person with a complete set of talents and capabilities. The problem with this partnership is that your complementary talents focus the pair of you on a single area of life, and this makes for not only a narrow outlook, but also a lack of flexibility in your response to changes. If the two of you are seeing everything in terms of career, or property, or personal freedom, or whatever, then you will have no way to deal effectively with a situation which cannot be dealt with in those terms. Life becomes like a seesaw; it alternates which end it has up or down, and can sometimes stay in balance; but it cannot swing round to face another way, and it is fixed to the ground so that it does not move.

These are the only combinations available, and all partnerships between two people can be described as a version of one of the seven types. It must be remembered, though, that some of the roles engendered by these dispositions of sign to sign are almost impossible to fulfil for some of the signs, because their essential energies, and the directions they are forced to take by the planets behind them, drive them in ways which make it too difficult. To form a relationship based on sharing and acceptance is one thing: to do it when you are governed by a planet like Mars is somethings else. Even when the relationship can form, the sort of approach produced by, say, Jupiter, is a very different thing from that produced by Venus.

The next thing you must consider, then, is how you, as a Capricorn, attempt relationships as a whole, and what you try to find in them. Then you must lay the qualities and outlook of each of the twelve signs over the roles they must play in the seven relationship types, and see whether the pair of you manage to make the best of that relationship, or not.

The seven relationship types are common to all the signs, relating to all the other signs. You can use your understanding of them to analyse and understand the relationship between any pair of people that you know, whether or not they are a Capricorn but to see how the characters fit into the framework in more detail, you will need to look at the individual compatibilities, of which just the Capricorn ones are given in this book.

The Capricorn Approach to Relationships

Because of the influence of Saturn, the Capricorn approaches relationships in a cautious manner, carefully considering the likely outcome of things before he commits himself. He forms friendships slowly, giving time for the acquaintance to deepen and develop; he is not the sort of person to rush blindly into a long-term commitment, or to fall in love over a single glass of wine.

If all that sounds dull, it has to be said that there is a good side to the idea of a Saturnine relationship, too. The good side consists of the strength and durability of the liaison once it is formed, and its resistance to outside attack. Some friendships are light things, and when circumstances separate the partners, the friendship dissolves; with Capricorns this doesn't happen. Once the friendship is formed, it will last for ever. Slow to form, but slow to dissolve—that's the way Saturn does things.

The essence of a relationship is its emotional content. The great love affairs, the ones which make history, are full of high passion and grand gestures, where the choices are either perfect bliss or utter destruction for both parties. Such passions appeal to Fire or Water sign people, but not to Capricorn. He doesn't really see the attraction in giving everything to an affair which distorts reality and makes impossible demands on the framework of normal life; indeed, he can see plenty of reasons why such strains and disruptions should be avoided.

For you, Capricorn, everything has to be in its place. Feelings are included in this scheme of things: you don't like your feelings to be loose, unrestrained, out of control, or public. You are a Saturnine person: you want them to be kept inside, out of public view. That doesn't mean that you are cold-hearted, but your feelings are small and tender, unlike the loud and, to you, tasteless, theatricalities indulged in by some Librans, for example. Also, unlike a Libran, whose very existence is determined by his relationships, they are not the most important thing in your life. You know this, and you are happy with the arrangement; everything in its place, according to you. Unfortunately the modern world and its media seem to place an unreasonable amount of emphasis on relationships, and they label you cold and unfeeling where you should really be termed tender and private.

You are, more than anything else, a builder. You like to build something out of your relationships, too—it would be unreasonable of you not to. When you enter a relationship with anyone, then, you are looking to see what you can build out of it, and you will do all that you can to make sure that the relationship is stable, structured, and useful. That is not to say that you spend your time cultivating useful business contacts instead of being genuinely friendly, though I dare say that some of you do exactly that, but you are well aware of how you want your friends to fit into the structure of your life nonetheless. Suppose, for example, that you have a friend who is your tennis partner. As far as you are concerned, you want to play tennis with him, and you want to chat to him about your game. You will never let him down when the pair of you have a match on, and you expect him to concentrate on his tennis as hard as you do. He isn't your business adviser, so you don't talk business to him, and he isn't somebody you share your personal worries with, so you don't confess your private fears to him. In other words, he is in a box in your life, marked 'Social: Tennis'. You will use one friend as a confidante, another as a financial adviser. It may well be that you are choosing these people for their professional skills as well as their personal qualities, but that is only because you prefer to deal with people who are recognized as being from the top of the pile—it is the Capricorn way.

Given this structured approach, a friend, in your eyes, must be somebody you can trust, somebody who is not going to change his view of you over the years, and somebody who is going to be a support to you when you need him to be. In return you will offer him similar qualities: staunch support, unwavering loyalty, reliability over a number of years. All very architectural, isn't it? That's the builder in you at work again. Other people may have friends who only last a few months, and then are never seen again, but not you. Youi are building a social life which will stand for a lifetime, and that needs solid foundations and good supports—not flighty friends.

Marriage is approached in a similarly architectural fashion. You are gloriously traditional about marriage—for you it lasts a lifetime. What you are looking for in a partner is somebody with whom you can build a future—that word again—and be stronger together than either of you were before. The ideal of this would be a marriage where both partners were equal in the power they held within the marriage, but this isn't often the case with you: you are too traditional for that. You prefer, in many instances, to be the senior partner, and to have your partner in a supporting role. This is because the aim of the Capricorn is to be at the top, and you reckon that if you can't achieve it on the small scale of your own home, you won't be able to manage it on the larger scale of public life. The argument is astrologically flawless, I'm afraid.

One of the prime aims of marriage, for the Capricornian, is to extend the family hierarchy. In other words, you uphold the traditional view that marriages are for mutual support and for children. Capricorns are quite good at having children; in fact they are a lot stronger sexually than they are usually given credit for. How can anybody whose sign is an old goat not be strongly sexed? Real sexual strength is present in all of the zodiac signs where the animal has horns—Aries, Taurus, and of course, Capricorn. The sexuality of the Capricorn is kept within the structure, agreed, but that doesn't mean it isn't there; it just means that the clever chat, the flamboyant display, and the paraphernalia of The Great Romance aren't there. The power itself is directed towards the advancement of the Capricorn within the structure, as with everything else in his life. That means the production of children within a marriage, and the development of the career outside it. Capricorn women are not above having affairs with their bosses to climb the hierarchy; perhaps more than any other sign, they understand that sex, money and power are all interchangeable.

Individual Compatibilities Sign by Sign

All relationships between the signs work in the ways described earlier in 'How Zodiacal Relationships Work'. In addition to that, descriptions of how a Capricorn attempts to form a relationship with someone from each of the twelve signs are given below. I have tried to show not what a Piscean, for example, is like, but what a Capricorn sees him as, and how he sees you. Each individual Piscean looks different, of course, but their motivation is the same, and these descriptions are meant to help you understand what you are trying to do with them, and how they are trying to handle you. As usual, the words he and his can be taken to mean she and her, since astrology makes no distinctions in sex here.

Capricorn-Aries
In the long run this relationship needs a fair bit of work if it is to be successful, though initially there are a lot of things you appear to have in common, and you will find that attractive. Both of you like to be effective in your actions, and you like to see things getting done rather than sit around thinking about them, but the motivation behind your preferences are very, very different.

The major difference between you is your idea of time. Aries lives for the instant: it is pretty difficult for him to imagine tomorrow with any degree of seriousness, let alone next year, and extreme cases may have difficulty with this afternoon, especially before lunch. You, on the other hand, can see next year as though it were today, and have no problems laying plans for five or even ten years hence. What you are doing is building for the future, while what he is doing is living for today. If you go into partnership with an Arian, you cannot expect him really to understand how important it is to you that things be done at the proper place and time; to them, if they want to do it, they will do it at once. Neither the future nor the past has any bearing on what an Arian does at this moment; only what he feels at this moment is of any importance. As you can see, his capacity for immediate action can be very useful for getting things started, but he needs (in your view, at any rate) careful guidance if his talents are not to be wasted, and if he is to help you realize your plans.

There is something very simple about an Arian, and it is rather noble at the same time: quite simply, he does things for the joy of doing them, not for the reward at the end. You know very well what makes you such a hard and willing worker is the recognition you hope to enjoy at the end of it all: in your world, the harder you work, the higher you rise.

Aries is simpler than that. He doesn't care what people think of his efforts. It never occurs to him to do something purely to enhance his reputation. He only knows whether the task at hand appeals to him—if it does, he will do it, and if it doesn't, he won't. What he actually works for is the pleasure of being at work; for him, the enjoyment he gets from experiencing action is as important as the pleasure you get when you are promoted to a new position. His whole existence is centred around the physical sensations of being in action. What he does something *for* doesn't matter—what matters is that he does it, and that he does it now. Aries is a pure physical force.

You appreciate his direct approach to things, his energy, and the fact that everything he attempts, he completes. You like his confidence, and his capacity for effort. If you had that kind of strength, you think, you could do anything. But there again, you remind yourself, that kind of explosive energy can only last a short time, and what you would really like is sustained energy over a longer period. What you want is steady heat, whereas the Arian provides ignition or explosion.

He sees you as a father figure. You have a longer view of events, and you are more sensible, in his eyes. You are surrounded by all the material tokens of seniority, and he sees you as older than you are because of them, and because it is obvious that you think and move much more slowly than he does. One day he would like to be like you—but not yet!

As friends, you will be pleased to find that you are aiming for the same goals. You will share a dislike for indecisive people, and an appreciation of anything that gives quick results from firm action. You will probably approve of each other's taste in cars and clothes, but for different reasons.

As lovers, you should be evenly matched. Capricorn has the stamina, while Aries has the strength; both of you come from the sign of an animal with horns, so you are both strongly sexed. Capricorns aren't usually very keen on experimental sex; strong but conventional is how you like it. As it happens, Arians are similar, because for them the body is more important than the mind, and so their imaginations aren't put to work thinking up variations; there will be few complaints from either of you.

As business partners, you could do very well provided that you channel his energy effectively; you will have to do the organizing for the two of you.

You would make a better marriage than many would think. Be prepared for the Arian's temper, and try at least sometimes to do things on the spur of the moment for his sake if nothing else. Essentially, you both appreciate each other's capabilities, and are willing to share your own in return for some of your partner's.

Capricorn-Taurus

This is a much easier relationship—one of your best. If stability and the enjoyment of your hard-earned high standard of living is what you want, then the Taurean is just the person to share it with you. They are an Earth sign, as you are, and so they understand instinctively the importance you place on what you have to show for your efforts. They appreciate beautiful things, too, and have similar tastes to yours.

Taureans are dedicated to steadiness, and the pursuit of a life without disturbance and change. When they are in a situation which seems both comfortable and manageable for them, they do all that they can to keep it as it is; they regard it as their particular territory, and will resist any attempts to dislodge them from it, defending it to the death, if need be.

What you like about Taureans is that they are the originators of the good life: sumptuously decorated houses, fine foods and wines, cars with leather seats and soft suspension are all Taurean. What a Taurean needs most of all is physical security, and by that he means surrounding himself with objects which he can touch and be comforted by. He needs to know where his next meal is coming from, and he needs that meal not only to nourish him, but to reassure him that he is as fine a person as he thinks he is, by its physical qualities. If you think about that for a moment, you will realize that not only must the Taurean have a very full freezer at all times, but it must be full of luxury food as well. If all he has to eat is basic foodstuffs, then he doesn't feel reassured. The same sort of ideas apply to his clothes and house as well.

To you, work is energy being converted into money; in the Taurean, you have a person whose existence is devoted to the appreciation of what that money will buy. You find that in itself reassuring, and when you wonder what you are working so hard for, five minutes with a Taurean will remind you.

The only problem with Taureans is that they are so static. You appreciate stability as much as anyone else, but you do like to feel yourself making progress and moving along through life; Taureans aren't interested in moving, only in making where they are more comfortable. There is a puritanical streak in you, which comes, unsurprisingly, from Saturn, and which enables you to do without life's little luxuries on the way to better things; Taurus won't do without *anything*.

They see you as exactly what they would like to be—financially successful. They miss the point to some extent, in that you are financially successful as a sort of side effect of being at the top of the pile, but that is entirely understandable because the idea of position doesn't have a lot of meaning for them. What they would like is to be able to afford all the lovely things they are so fond of—and it seems that you have the ability to turn time into money, which is true.

As friends, you will enjoy each other's company immensely, and will particularly enjoy spending money together; they will find your sense of the status of objects as interesting as you find their sense of texture and colour. You could both end up extremely fat, of course; food is a major pleasure with Taureans. When matters get serious, though, and you need to discuss your next move, you will seek advice from elsewhere; their defensive approach to business isn't always what you want to hear. Should you go into business together, they make wonderful partners, because they will always be supportive and reliable; the initiative, however, has to come from you.

Although having a lover of the same element as yourself is usually a good thing, you might find that they are more sensitive emotionally than you had realized, and you could be out of your depth a little. On a sexual level you may be surprised by their strength and possessiveness.

This pairing makes for a good marriage provided that your main aim is to have a secure and enjoyable home life; if you are more interested in achieving than enjoying you will find the Taurean more of a hindrance than a help.

Capricorn-Gemini

This is a very dry and crackly sort of pairing: there are plenty of things to produce sparks between you, but almost no heat. Emotionally, this one is conducted at a very low level, and because of that it may be the sort of thing you are looking for.

Gemini has the fastest thinking brain in the whole zodiac. He is able to see the point of a sentence before the speaker has finished. He also likes re-telling stories, with slightly altered details, just for fun. He can play with words and ideas like nobody else, and he doesn't really believe any one of them. This isn't surprising: Nature makes ducks waterproof because they spend a lot of time in the water, and it makes Geminis immune to persuasion by the words they use so much.

What a Gemini needs more than anything else is to be amused, and he does this by absorbing huge amounts of new information. He doesn't remember it all, and he doesn't want to: he just wants to read it or hear it, and for it to keep him amused for a few minutes.

He is not working to a plan in the same way that you are, though he does have a better sense of time than, say, an Arian. He isn't part of a structure, either; he doesn't feel that everything is best if it stays in its appointed place. There is a strong streak of the anarchist in a Gemini, which rises to the surface every so often when he feels that things aren't changing fast enough to keep him amused, and that he had better do something about it.

Geminis don't share your belief that hard work is the only way to achieve your goals, either. They are, given half a chance, extremely lazy. It's not really their fault—they are an Air sign, which isn't at all practical or down-to-earth, and they are governed by Mercury, which doesn't have the weight or driving force of, say, Saturn or Mars.

So far, it seems you are trying to form a relationship with an idle, fork-tongued anarchist; what is it about them that captivates you? Firstly, his sense of humour. Geminian humour is all verbal and cerebral; there is very little of the simple clown in it. Your own sense of humour is wry and dry, and his sharp wit appeals to you a great deal. Because of the Saturnine influence you bring with you, in your presence his humour becomes even more piercing and sardonic, and in return your own becomes more verbal and better expressed. The pity about this process is that the lighter side of the Gemini's humour, the awful schoolboy jape side, gets lost; you have no time for that sort of thing, and so your Saturn influence crushes it out of the Gemini before it gets a chance to show itself.

The other thing you like about Geminians is their ability to analyse situations at work. They are fast, accurate, and dispassionate, and you admire them for it. If you were like that, you think,you could really make some progress. It never occurs to you that Gemini isn't interested in that sort of progress, does it?

They see you as rather slow, and too careful by half, but they like your black humour, and they would like to enjoy the capacity for self-indulgence that your financial success brings with it. As long as you continue to move up, and to be with powerful people, the Gemini will stay around to be entertained.

As friends, the main attraction is that you are both unemotional; neither of you is likely to get sentimental about the other, and you are both thankful for that. You are much stronger sexually than the Gemini, so if you should become lovers you will be the dominant partner. If you keep things varied, the Gemini will perform well enough; become serious or obsessive, though, and he will quickly lose interest.

As business partners you are wonderful together, provided that your ambition is strong enough to override any twinges of conscience arising from the Gemini's *very* sharp deals.

Marriage? Yes, if you make a few allowances for each other. The flavour of the marriage is hard, though, like bare furniture: fine if you like that sort of thing, but most people like cushions now and again.

Capricorn-Cancer

This is the union of opposites, and as is always the case in astrology (and real life too), you have a lot more in common than you would think.

Cancer, like you, is concerned with the structure of things. He is reserved, polite, and proper in his dealings, as you are, and mindful of the rights and requirements of others, as you are also. He is a collecting sign, as you are, and is therefore concerned with taking in energy from others so that he can strengthen his own position. Finally, he is a Cardinal sign, as you are, and so he thinks that he won't get anywhere unless he does something about it personally.

Familiar, isn't it? The difference is that his world is internal where yours is external. His purpose and aim is to protect what is his from the attentions of the world, whereas yours is to have the world applaud you for what you have achieved.

Imagine that everyone was given a large box to help them live their life. You, Capricorn, would have the outside of the box painted in fashionable colours, and decked out in fabrics which would show off your status to everybody. This done, you would climb on top of the box so that everybody could see that you were higher up than they were. Now consider Cancer.

Cancer would live inside the box. The outside would be completely plain and featureless; unremarkable and uninviting. Not hostile, not rude, but private nonetheless. Inside would be the most comfortable and cosy home you could imagine, where the whole family would live their lives with much love and affection. The purpose of it all would be emotional nourishment, support, and protection.

The box represents the structure of your life and your career, of course. To you, it exists for you to be able to get to the top; for the Cancer, it exists for his reassurance.

Neither of you can live without that structure. Both of you find it the essential feature of your lives, and if it is ever dissolved, you will build another one at once, in much the same way as spiders with webs.

Cancer has the same sense of time as you do, and is interested in working towards the far future in a patient fashion. You are both builders: he is interested in laying the foundations, and you are interested in the topping-off, but you are both builders at heart, and you can appreciate it in each other.

He sees you as rather too public in your tastes, and uncomfortably spartan and self-denying in your personal life, but he welcomes your serious approach to getting on in life.

You see him as a bit of a worrier, and a little too sentimental about things to be a really effective decision-maker, but you appreciate his determination to succeed. You also welcome his belief that the traditional way of things is probably the best.

As friends, you will take time to get to know one another; once you have each other's trust, the friendship will last for ever.

As lovers, you will find that the Cancerian is as strong as you are, but in different ways; you will find his emotional needs difficult to respond to at first.

In business, you should do well, though you are both better suited to rising through a big organization than to starting up on your own.

Marriage between you is a good idea, because it is a long-term thing, and both of you work better over a longer period. You must appreciate how vital the Cancerian's home life is to him, though.

Capricorn-Leo

You don't find Fire signs enjoyable: this partnership, along with the Sagittarian one, is easily the most difficult of the twelve for you. Put quite simply, Leos make you spit.

They are lazy, good-natured souls, and they seem to be well-liked for it. You can understand being liked for working, but not for being idle; the fact that they seem to be able to do exactly that annoys you. It never occurs to you that you can't buy affection, that being pleasant isn't to do with being rich, or that hard work won't necessarily make you popular, but that's just how you are—that's the disadvantage of being an Earth sign, and you knew that there had to be one somewhere.

You know what confidence is; it's that inner warmth that comes from being in control, being right, and being able to afford to do what you like. You have it, in some measure, and the harder you work, the more of it you hope to get. It's expensive stuff, as far as you're concerned, because it is only achieved in return for much labour; but there again, if it didn't cost you a lot to get it, you wouldn't feel that it was valuable, would you?

Leos were born with it. They have warmth, confidence, and affability enough to throw away—and they do. The sheer waste of it all offends you. How can they be like that, you cry—though what you really mean is why can't I be like that?

The truth of the matter is that you are jealous of Leos. Leo represents the Sun, the source of light and heat, the centre of the solar system. Against their light, you are thrown into shadow. Saturn's weight, the source of your power, is made to seem what it is in the Leo's sunshine—small, cold, grey, and dull. Your achievements are all external: inside you are still the same as you were when you started. What you have managed to do is to compel admiration and respect for your position, but that can't compete with somebody who gives out warmth and light for free. Basically, Leo's make you look like Scrooge, and you don't like it.

They see you as somebody out to usurp their position as the natural centre of the group. They see your structured approach to life as being rather unimaginative and cold, and they would rather not give time to it. Life is one big party to a Leo, but they have to have an audience, and they have to be the star of the of the show; if you look as though you will threaten that then they will be most displeased. There is a sense of nobility about Leos: they show royal displeasure if they feel that they are not given due recognition.

A friendship between you is going to be something of a power struggle: both of you want the other to admit that you are the prominent partner. The way round it is to give the Leo preference in a social and personal context, and to concentrate your own power in the world of finance and business. The only trouble here is that neither of you will pay much attention to the other's sphere of influence, since you both rate the other's as unimportant and trivial. The power struggle continues on a physical level if you become lovers.

As business partners you could do a lot for each other. Leo has the confidence, and the capacity to inspire confidence, that you often lack. Leo doesn't have your capacity for hard work, or anything like it, but he has an organizational ability which will surprise you when you first meet it. After a while you will recognize that it is as effective and reliable as your own—and considerably more flexible! He hasn't your touch with money, though, so you'll have to look after that for him.

Your marriage would certainly be fun to watch. You would live in the finest style, and have some memorable rows when you felt that your partner was being too selfish. It would need a lot of adjustment from both of you to be really successful, though it would be strengthened by children. Leos love children generally, and are natural parents. Both of you have dynastic ambitions, and see children as extensions of your own excellence going on to the next generation; your own children would give you a common goal.

Capricorn-Virgo

Here is the second pairing from within your own element. It is much lighter in tone than the Taurean one, and less of its energy is converted into physical objects. From your point of view, it is quite a thought-provoking relationship, and one in which you feel quite comfortable.

The emotional force of Taurus is absent here; Venus' romantic energies are replaced by the altogether cooler ones of Mercury, and you are probably happier with the swap.

Virgo, like Gemini, is a clever and analytical thinker. In this case the mental talents are directed to practical ends, as you would expect for an Earth sign, and the result is an analysis of processes and techniques rather than words and ideas. Virgos are experts on how to do things; they know what to do, how to do it, what skills and tools are needed, and how to add extra little touches to get the result they want. When they meet something new they will take it to pieces to see how it works—sometimes literally! They are thoughtful and methodical in their approach; they like to understand a thing fully and thoroughly, right down to the level of its components, before they feel at home with it.

You will appreciate all this, and feel reassured by the Virgoan approach. There are times when you are working so hard that you don't have time to think, or when you know what has to be done but you aren't sure why it has to be done that way; Virgo tells you the reasons why, and it all makes sense to you.

You have to believe in the order of things: if they are not in their places, if there is no structure and pattern, then you are lost. Virgo reminds you that the order of things carries on down to the smallest level, right down to molecular level, if need be, and you find that very comforting.

On a personal level, you are one of the few people who find Virgo's methodical approach praiseworthy, and his obsession with getting things exactly right admirable. Most people find him picky and over-critical.

He finds your success an inspiring thought. He can see that you work in a similar way, but on a larger scale to himself, and if he had the time and energy he would be just like you, he feels sure. Whenever he has doubts about the correctness of his approach, he looks at what hard work has brought you and feels pleased.

Given that you find each other mutually admirable, a friendship is likely to form very quickly. You fit together very well indeed: he will try constantly to do things for you, and you will be proud of him for it. It is, in fact, his way of showing his affection. He cannot express himself with soft sentiment; instead he shows his affection by being useful. Being useful is the finest thing he can imagine, just as being successful is your fondest dream; if he is useful to you, and you are made more successful because of it, then you have the makings of a fulfilling relationship, though not all of the signs would recognize it as such.

As lovers, you will find that the absence of any sense of the romantic produces a rather dry and dutiful relationship. Virgos are critical of any process which they think could be done better—mind your self-esteem as you get into bed!

You would make a good partnership in business. Virgos can't always see the whole situation at once, but you can; there again, you sometimes can't see the details of things, but that's just what they're best at. You compensate for each other's deficiencies beautifully, and you both enjoy the actual process of working. A really winning combination.

The same sense of industry and purpose would go into a marriage between you, and that would make it a success in material terms. The relationship would lack emotional warmth, though, and it could be seriously short of laughter. You both take life too seriously at times.

Capricorn-Libra

A very interesting combination. You are two very different people, but each of you has a major talent that the other finds highly desirable, and that's what gives the relationship its initial impetus.

Librans are not practical people like Virgoans. They deal in words and ideas, like all the Air signs; they don't care how a thing gets done so long as they like it when it is finished. In fact, Librans care a great deal about how a thing looks, and they care even more that it should look attractive.

This is the thing that captivates you about a Libran: they have *taste*. They have other qualities, too, but you react most strongly to the ones which apply to your world, and you understand material things much more easily than you understand ideas and feelings. Librans have the ability to choose the most graceful, the most elegant, the most pleasing to the eye, time and time again; you, on the other hand, can't seem to get a lot further than deciding what you want and how much you are going to pay for it. Once your life has been touched by a Libran, compliments start to come rolling in, and you are very keen for that to start happening, very keen indeed.

Librans are professionally nice people: there isn't anyone who doesn't like them. This quality, instant likability, as you see it, is very attractive to you; it makes you rather ashamed of your own rather low social profile, and your own reputation for being too serious.

There are disadvantages to being everything to everybody, though, and one of them is that you have to keep changing your mind. Indecisiveness isn't something that ever troubles you, and it is that very thing which makes the Libran so eager to make your acquaintance. If some of your firmness of purpose, sense of organization or simply hardness of exterior could be transferred to the Libran, he would be delighted. He is never certain which course to take, never able to decide what to do next for the best, and never able to say no to anybody if he thinks that they might be upset. All of these weaknesses are very apparent to him, as is the fact that you have none of them, and he would love to change places with you.

There are drawbacks to the partnership: just because you admire certain qualities in each other doesn't mean that everything else slips into place, you know. Libra is likely to find you rather serious; he would like you better if you laughed more often, and if you shared his pleasure in going out and being among friends. You would like him to be firmer in his approach to things which demand it; at times he can be impossibly lightweight, and it just makes you sigh with frustration.

A friendship between you is going to be either on or off. In many cases your interests won't coincide to a great enough extent for you even to think about seeing any more of each other than you have to; but on other occasions you will feel that you get enough out of each other for you to ignore your differences. In the best instances you will admire what the other one is trying to do: Capricorn will understand the importance of the intimate personal relationship to the Libran, and the Libran will understand the Capricorn's need to be seen as the best.

A sexual relationship between you would be a lot more successful than you might think, given that friendship itself is so difficult to achieve. Librans have just a hint of coolness somewhere in that impeccable style, a suggestion of vanity which means that they are always making sure that they are looking good rather than giving themselves totally to the experience. Capricorns understand this; it is part of their nature too. You can build a very exciting sexual partnership out of that, provided that you don't do things *too* publicly and get yourselves arrested, of course.

A business partnership isn't really Libra's sort of thing, or at least not in the same way that it is for the Capricorn. Marriage, on the other hand, is a very Libran thing. Try this one, Capricorn, and you will have a stylish home but a lazy partner—because once the relationship is permanent the Libran's purpose is complete!

Capricorn-Scorpio

This is the easiest of them all, from your point of view. There are some pairings in the zodiac which fit together so closely that the joins are invisible, and the combined strength of the two is more than twice their single strength. One of the partnerships (there are only two) is Taurus and Cancer, and the other one is this. It isn't a comfortable partnership, either to be in or to handle from the outside, but it certainly achieves its aims. It is ruthless, dominant, and wonderfully effective.

Scorpio is interested in the maintenance of power and control. To him, knowing how people are likely to react is essential intelligence; when he has this intelligence he can control the entire situation. Everything that a Scorpio attempts is done with tremendous power, directed in precisely the right way to ensure the desired result. They are secretive people, and they go to great lengths to keep their own movements hidden; they also go to great lengths to determine and discover the hidden movements of everybody else.

As you can see, they are very powerful, yet very private; you are different in that you want to be in power and publicly recognized for it. Different aims, but not all that far apart; certainly there is much that you have in common, and you are close enough in outlook to enjoy each other's company.

Scorpio is trying to be powerful, and you are trying to be in a position of power: one is a condition of potential, the other an established state. You represent what happens when the Scorpio's power is converted into material wealth, and he represents the invisible network of influence which later becomes crystallized into the organizational structure you love so much.

He sees you as being the steady state of permanent control, very much the sort of thing that he admires. He is seeing the weight of Saturn, in fact, which restricts and encloses. He himself works through Mars, that irresistible force applied suddenly and to one point, and so he hasn't got your stamina or your patience; you haven't got his immediate power, though, so it balances out.

You are not likely to be friends so much as co-conspirators: you will have a special vocabulary of codewords and symbols, each of which refers to people in positions of power and their position in your schemes. From the outside, it seems impenetrable, untrustworthy, and generally hostile; inside the partnership, though, you are having a glorious time. This is the only relationship which has what you would no doubt describe as a properly professional and serious outlook on life. It is also the only one where the other partner is at least as ambitious as you are.

You don't generally mix business and your emotions; be doubly careful with the Scorpio, whose business is emotions. He will be as cool and businesslike as you are, but he will be playing with your emotions the whole while. You will see just how important they are to him if you develop your friendship into an affair, and you will also be introduced to the full force of Mars. Scorpio will knock you flat, sexually, though it is comforting to know that eventually, after a very long time, you will prove to be the stronger of the two, simply because of your greater capacity for endurance. It will take too much out of you to find out, though; don't try to match him if you argue on this subject.

As business partners, you were made for each other. There ought to be a law against business partnerships of this sort, to give the others a chance.

As marriage partners, you should be reasonably suited. You will need to be in the seat at the head of the table, but he will actually be in control, because marriages are emotional things, and that's where he is stronger. If he gets obsessive about something, you will have to let him win, because he will break up all that you have built together rather than lose, and you wouldn't want that.

Capricorn-Sagittarius

After the pairing which is closest to yourself comes the one which is the furthest away. Like Leos, Sagittarians seem to embody all the things you would rather not come into contact with, and being with them just brings out the worst in you. And yet they are irresistible: there is something engaging about them which you feel drawn to, and wish that you weren't.

Sagittarians are open and optimistic people; to them everything is full of life and interest, and they like nothing better than to have something new and untried to look into. They are insatiably curious, and childishly trusting; in their world there are no hidden pitfalls, and even if there are they know that they will come to no harm.

All of this you can tolerate quite easily; to you it seems simply that they are rather young in their outlook, and you find yourself adopting a parental role with them. You indulge their enthusiasm with an avuncular twinkle in your eye, and they play up to it.

What is less easy for you to tolerate is their knowledge. Sagittarians seem to have been born wise beyond their years, and they already know all that there is to know about everything before you even open a conversation with them. Once you do, they assume that you would like to know what they know, and they tell you. They are bubbling over with knowledge; they simply can't keep it all to themselves. This is a bit hard for you to take: you have fairly traditional views on education, and it goes against the grain to be told where you are going wrong by somebody who behaves like a five-year old with a new toy the whole time. What makes things worse is they're usually right.

The most incomprehensible thing of all about Sagittarians is their insistence on freedom and movement. They won't let themselves settle down and put down roots the way you think that they should. The very idea of staying in the same job, or doing the same thing, for years on end, the way you do, makes them feel faint, and quite often they will change jobs, or even careers, for no other reason than that they have been doing the same thing for over three years, and it bothers them.

You know how fond you are of a structured and ordered existence, and how you see the rules and regulations of a formal lifestyle as a solid framework on which to build? Sagittarians are just the opposite. They are frightened of frameworks, because to their eyes every framework looks like a cage. Being trapped is their greatest fear: they are never afraid of anything new, but the thought of never changing from something that they don't like terrifies them. You, of course, would always prefer an eternity of something that you knew, no matter how bad it was, to the possibility of the unknown and untried.

You see them as childish, charming, infuriatingly clever, and short of staying-power; they see you as successful and powerful, but lacking in sparkle, and far too hardworking for your own health.

A friendship between you is likely to be built on a sense of mutual fascination: most probably the Sagittarian will take you on as a project, attempting to inject what he sees as necessary gaiety into your life, while you will feel that he needs calming down and directing, and will attempt to do that for him. If you succeed, you will quench the fire in him completely; it is actually a better thing if you allow yourself to be taken along with him on some of his adventures—as long as you stay close to him you will come to no harm.

A Sagittarian lover will be everything you could want for as long as he retains his interest in you; they get bored after a while and start looking around for somebody new. Not better, just new—there's no question of not making the grade, it's just that novelty is a big factor in attracting a Sagittarian.

Pick somebody else as a business partner: Sagittarians are rarely interested in high finance. Money doesn't seem as real to them as it does to you, and the work required to make a lot of it simply isn't worth it to them.

Marrying a Sagittarian is actually a very smart move from your point of view, provided that you don't stifle them. They are always warm and forward-looking, which is a big bonus in a life-long relationship, but for them to maintain this outlook you must be flexible, and not try to tie them down too much.

Capricorn-Capricorn

Forming a relationship with somebody of your own sign is easy on the surface, because you should know what you're getting. There are a few of the same-sign combinations, though, which don't work as well as they should because it is part of the nature of the sign to resent competition, and that can happen here.

The only drawback to this relationship is that both of you are striving to get to the top; if the relationship is the most important thing in your lives, then one of you has to lose somewhere, and that will cause resentment. There is an easy way round the problem, though, and it is one which most Capricorn partners employ without even thinking about it.

It is simply not to let the relationship be the most important thing in your life. Most Capricorns are far more interested in their work than they are in their private lives anyway, and rightly so, since public success rather than private happiness is your eventual goal. Besides, you can always pack your private affairs into a separate compartment of your life, and give them some time and attention when you get a spare minute; they needn't interfere with your career at all.

Your only problem in the past has been to find somebody who understands all this, somebody who will give you support when you need it, somebody who is as keen to succeed as you are, and who will understand if you are too busy to give them any time when they may need it. This person will have to be at least as tough as you are, at least as able to endure emotional hardship, and at least as able to sacrifice the comforts and pleasures of the present for the rewards of the future. What they will have to be is another Capricorn.

Having another Capricorn as a partner in any sense means that they understand your motivation, and will make allowances automatically for those times when you are too busy to be sociable, and when other signs would say you were being miserable or rude.

It sounds a good idea on the surface, but it means that the relationship will have a very low emotional content; how could it be otherwise? If you want warmth, love, and affection in your life, to compensate for those qualities which you know that you are short of, then don't choose another version of yourself to supply them. On the other hand, if you really are dedicated to getting on in life, and you don't feel comfortable with intangible things like sentiment and affection, then this will no doubt suit you. If you do choose this partnership, then you will both be supporting each other in your struggles, and indeed as the years pass the relationship will become a sort of achievement factory. Both of you will rise higher and higher in your chosen professions, gaining more and more of that Capricornian product, money.

As a light friendship, this pairing has little time to say more than a few words as they pass in the lift at the office, but as a life partnership, either in business or as a marriage, it is much more productive, as we have already seen. The key element is, of course, time: Capricorn does everything best over the long period, and relationships are just the same.

Sexually, the success of the relationship depends on how much time you are prepared to give to this side of it. Sex, power, money, and status are interchangeable to you, and it will be very satisfying to you to have a partner who understands this without being told. This could be the only sexual pairing where you can really express your understanding of sex and power, and where you won't be putting your partner off.

Capricorn-Aquarius

The sign which is one stage further on in the zodiacal cycle from your own is always enticing but elusive. Usually it represents some sort of idea which is beyond your capabilities, and is governed by a planet whose energies are very different from your own. In this case the difference between you is considerably lessened by the fact that you are both looked after by the same planet, Saturn.

You know what you are going to find in another Saturnine individual, and that familiarity before the event, so to speak, gives you confidence. They are going to be reserved, unemotional, a bit cool. Yes, they are, but in every other respect they are vastly different from you. The things which will hit you hardest are firstly that they are very friendly and sociable, which you are not, on the whole, and secondly, that they are very firmly opposed to the idea of anybody being in a position of power over anybody else.

This will confuse you. Surely Saturn will give them some sense of structure, you think. Indeed it does: but in the opposite direction to yours. You are concerned with vertical structures, where every person is at a different height from everybody else, and the direction of movement is up or down. Aquarius is concerned with horizontal structures, where everybody is at the same level, and connected in a network of friendship and shared interests. The direction of movement is out, through, or along.

Aquarius is an Air sign, which means that they are working with words and ideas, a realm in which you are not at home. You can understand the Aquarian's version of the Air element better than you could with Gemini and Libra, though, because it is Fixed here, and therefore less likely to slip through your fingers. If you watch an Aquarian in action in any social gathering, you will be able to see how similar he is to you. The only reason you have not seen it before is that you are so much at sea in any sort of personal or emotional situation that you think them all to be the same. In fact, each group and each party is different, and if you watch the Aquarian you will be able to see how he handles people with the same practised ease that you handle money.

He is always at the centre of the discussion, but he is never attached to one particular person. The party seems to flow round him, but he is never moved along by it. Although he is very much part of the crowd, he is not of the same stuff as the crowd; he is just a little bit different, separate, distanced almost.

That same distance is there in his eyes, if you look: he knows what he's doing the whole time. He's not heartless, and he's not calculating or manipulative as a Scorpio is, but he doesn't let himself get carried away unless he wants it to be that way. It's as though he's ballasted, so that he always floats and always stays upright. In fact, he *is* ballasted—by Saturn.

Once you have seen how cool he is, and how he keeps himself separate and different from all his friends, whilst being a good friend to all of them, you will be hooked. Here is somebody, you will say to yourself, who is as professional in his social life as I am in my business life.

There's more to him than that, actually; he has high principles, humanitarian politics, and a determinedly modernist outlook on life which doesn't fit at all with your cherished ideals of tradition and privilege. You will fight over these things as your friendship deepens. You may see him as cool and stylish, but he sees you as self-centred, over-conventional, and an opponent of progress. It is always much more difficult to think kindly of the sign behind you than the one in front of you, mainly because the sign behind you shows you your own bad side in some respects—some

Aquarians are mercenary enough to trade their principles for hard cash, which is very Capricornian!

Because he is cool, and you are often too busy to give the time to such things, you may not develop a sexual relationship at all; even if you do, it will be characterized by its cool, almost 'blue' (in a jazz sense) flavour rather than by intense passions.

Aquarius isn't likely to be quite the business partner of your dreams, though his social skills could undoubtedly be put to good use; like all the Air signs, he isn't really at home in fixed routines where the product is more important than the people—he prefers it the other way round.

As a marriage partner he is a much better bet. He is cool enough not to make emotional demands upon you, and independent enough to have things to do when you are working late; the question is, though, are you really interested enough in each other to marry in the first place?

Capricorn-Pisces

This is as unlikely a combination as you could ever imagine, and yet it works surprisingly well; you couldn't wish for a less structured and less ambitious person than a Piscean, yet they seem to welcome you, and you seem to enjoy their very changeability. How does this come about?

Partly it is because of their extreme sensitivity. You are not very good at expressing yourself, and you only give the merest hints when you think that you are opening your heart to the world. Pisceans are sensitive enough to pick up the little that you offer, and respond to it in a big enough way for you to gain emotional satisfaction from it. Their response, though genuine, is in no way forceful or enveloping, however, and it will break over you like a wave on the shore, leaving you unchanged—and that's just how you want it. What you want is somebody who can respond to your needs, but whose response doesn't throw you off course in any way, or stop you from doing what you see as your work. Pisceans fit the bill. There is a lot of emotion in a Capricorn, but it is slow and deep, like the ocean—the Capricorn animal has the tail of a fish, remember—and Pisces is the only

Water sign further on in the zodiac than Capricorn; therefore it is the only one through which the Capricorn can express that energy.

On any other level than the emotional, Pisceans are just the same as you are. To be fair, they are just the same as anybody else in the zodiac, because they are able to take on the qualities of the person they are with at the time, through a process of absorption and reflection. This means that while they are involved with you, they are just as ambitious and hard-headed.

Most of the time Pisceans are unsure of which direction to take. The fact that you are very sure of where you are going is attractive to them; while they are with you they can become part of your life and take your firmness of direction on themselves. It means, of course, that they are then heading in the same direction as you are, but they don't care too much about where they are going, as long as they are going somewhere.

You mustn't expect them to be able to be firm on their own account; what happens is that you take the decisions, and they mimic you. Left to their own devices, they probably won't do things forcefully enough, and you will find that some of your schemes are starting to come loose at the edges; only you have the power and the authority necessary to hold things the way you want them. At the same time, if you control their actions too closely, they will be unhappy and try to escape—Piscean fish are very sensitive to any sort of pressure, and it causes them a lot of pain.

Friendship between you is likely to be formed from a basis of mutual emotional sympathy: if you keep it at that level, without trying to control or restrict them, then the friendship should prove satisfying to you both. If you become lovers, then you will have to make allowances for their changeable moods, and they will have to allow for your lack of imagination (by their standards)!

You could do wonders in business with a Piscean if you are in any kind of media business; they just slip right in. Marriage probably isn't such a good idea, though; they will want more of your time than you are prepared to spare them.

Part 3

Your Life

5. The Year within Each Day

You have probably wondered, in odd moments, why there are more than twelve varieties of people. You know more than twelve people who look completely different. You also know more than one person with the same Sun sign as yourself who doesn't look anything like you. You also know two people who look quite like each other, but who are not related, and do not have birthdays near each other, so can't be of the same Sun sign. You will have come to the conclusion that Sun signs and astrology don't work too well, because anyone can see that there are more than twelve sorts of people.

You will also have wondered, as you finished reading a newspaper or magazine horoscope, how those few sentences manage to apply to a twelfth of the nation, and why it is that they are sometimes very close to your true circumstances, and yet at other times miles off. You will have come to the conclusion that astrology isn't all that it might be, but some of it is, and that you like it enough to buy magazines for the horoscopes, and little books like this one.

It might be that there is some other astrological factor, or factors, which account for all the different faces that people have, the similarities between people of different Sun signs, and the apparent inconsistencies in magazine horoscopes. There are, indeed, lots of other astrological factors we could consider, but one in particular will answer most of the inconsistencies we have noticed so far.

It is the Ascendant, or rising sign. Once you know your Ascendant, you will see how you get your appearance, your way of working, your tastes, your preferences and dislikes, and your state of health (or not, as the case may be). It is perhaps of more use to you to consider yourself as belonging to your Ascendant sign, than your Sun sign. You have been reading the wrong newspaper horoscopes for years; you are not who you thought you were!

You are about to protest that you know when your birthday is. I'm sure you do. This system is not primarily linked to your birthday, though. It is a smaller cogwheel in the clockwork of the heavens, and we must come down one level from where we have been standing to see its movements. Since astrology is basically the large patterns of the sky made small in an individual, there are a number of 'step-down' processes where the celestial machinery adjusts itself to the smaller scale of mankind; this is one of them.

Here's the theory:

Your birthday pinpoints a particular time during the year. The Sun appears to move round the strip of sky known as the zodiac during the course of the year. In reality, of course, our planet, Earth, moves round the Sun once a year, but the great friendly feature of astrology is that it always looks at things from our point of view; so, we think we stand still, and the Sun appears to move through the zodiac. On a particular day of importance, such as your birthday, you can see which of the zodiac signs the Sun is in, pinpoint how far it has gone in its annual trip round the sky, and then say 'This day is important to me, because it is my birthday; therefore this part of the sky is important to me because the Sun is there on my special day. What are the qualities of that part of the Sun's journey through the zodiac, and what are they when related to me?' The answer is what you usually get in a horoscope book describing your Sun sign.

Fine. Now let's go down one level, and get some more detail. The Earth rotates on its own axis every day. This means that, from our point of view, we stand still and the sky goes round us once a day. Perhaps you hadn't thought of it before, but that's how the Sun appears to move up and across the sky from sunrise to sunset. It's actually us who are moving, but we see it the other way round. During any day, then, your birthday included, the whole of the sky goes past you at some time or another; but at a particular moment of importance, such as the time that you were born, you can see where the Sun is, see which way up the sky is, and say, 'This moment is important to me, because I was born at this time; therefore the layout of the sky has the same qualities as I do. What are the qualities of the sky at this time of day, and what are they when related to me?'

You can see how you are asking the same questions one level lower down. The problem is that you don't know which bit of the sky is significant. Which bit do you look at? All you can see? All that you can't (it's spherical from your point of view, and has no joins; half of it is below the horizon, remember)?

How about directly overhead? A very good try; the point in the zodiac you would arrive at is indeed significant, and is used a lot by astrologers, but there is another one which is more useful still. The eastern horizon is the point used most. Why? Because it fulfils more functions than any other point. It gives a starting point which is easily measurable, and is even visible (remember, all astrology started from observations made before mathematics or telescopes). It is also the contact point between the sky and the earth, from our point of view, and thus symbolizes the relationship between the sky and mankind on the earth. Finally, it links the smaller cycle of the day to the larger one of the year, because the Sun starts its journey on the eastern horizon each day as it rises; and, if we are concerned with a special moment, such as the time of your birth, then the start of the day, or the place that it started, at any rate, is analogous to the start of your life. Remember that you live the qualities of the moment you were born for all of your life; you are that moment made animate.

The point in the zodiac, then, which was crossing the eastern horizon at the time you were born, is called the Ascendant. If this happened to be somewhere in the middle of Gemini, then you have a Gemini Ascendant, or Gemini rising, whichever phrase you prefer. You will see that this has nothing to do with the time

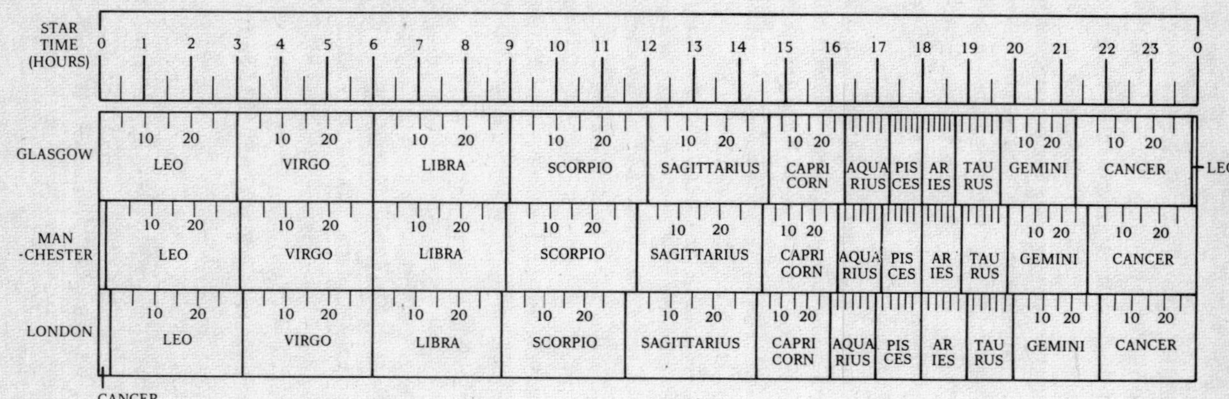

Different signs are on the horizon at different times according to where you live, as you can see. This is because of the difference in latitude. If you live in between the places given, you can make a guess from the values here. To compensate for longitude, subtract twelve minutes from your birthtime if you live in Glasgow, Liverpool or Cardiff; ten minutes for Edinburgh or Manchester, and six minutes for Leeds, Tyneside, or the West Midlands. *Add* four minutes for Norwich.

of year that you were born, only with the time of day.

Have a look at the diagram opposite, which should help explain things. If two people are born on the same day, but at different times, then the Ascendant will be different, and the Sun and all the other planets will be occupying different parts of the sky. It makes sense to assume, then, that they will be different in a number of ways. Their lives will be different, and they will look different. What they will have in common is the force of the Sun in the same sign, but it will show itself in different ways because of the difference in time and position in the sky.

How do you know which sign was rising over the eastern horizon when you were born? You will have to work it out. In the past, the calculation of the Ascendant has been the subject of much fuss and secrecy, which astrologers exploit to the full, claiming that only they can calculate such things. It does take some doing, it is true, but with a few short cuts and a calculator it need only take five minutes.

Here is the simplest routine ever devised for you to calculate your own Ascendant, provided that you know your time of birth. Pencil your answers alongside the stages as you go, so you know where you are.

1. Count forwards from 22 December to your birthday: 22 December is 1, 23 December is 2, and so on.
   Total days: ....
2. Add 92 to this. New total is: ....
3. Divide by 365, and then
4. Multiply by 24. Answer is now: ....
   (Your answer by now is between 0 and 24. If it isn't, you have made a mistake somewhere. Go back and try again.)
5. Add your time of birth, in 24-hour clock time. If you were born at 3 p.m., that means 15. If you were born in Summer Time, take one hour off. If there are some spare minutes, your calculator would probably like them in decimals, so it's 0.1 of an hour for each six minutes. 5.36 p.m. is 17.6, for example. Try to be as close as you can. New total is: ....

6. If your total exceeds 24, subtract 24. Your answer must now be between 0 and 24. Answer is: ....
7. You have now got the time of your birth not in clock time, but in sidereal, or star, time, which is what astrologers work in. Page 72 has a strip diagram with the signs of the Zodiac arranged against a strip with the values 0 to 24, which are hours in star time. Look against the time you have just calculated, and you will see which sign was rising at the time you were born. For example, if your calculated answer is 10.456, then your Ascendant is somewhere in the middle of 10.456, then your Ascendant is about the 16th degree of Scorpio.

What Does the Ascendant Do?

Broadly speaking, the Ascendant does two things. Firstly, it gives you a handle on the sky, so that you know which way up it was at the time you entered the game, so to speak; this has great significance later on in the book, when we look at the way you handle large areas of activity in your life such as your career, finances, and ambitions. Secondly, it describes your body. If you see your Sun sign as your mentality and way of thinking, then your Ascendant sign is your body and your way of doing things. Think of your Sun sign as the true you, but the Ascendant as the vehicle you have to drive through life. It is the only one you have, so you can only do with it the things of which it is capable, and there may be times when you would like to do things in a different way, but it 'just isn't you'. What happens over your life is that your Sun sign energies become specifically adapted to express themselves to their best via your Ascendant sign, and you become an amalgam of the two. If you didn't, you would soon become very ill. As a Capricorn with, say, a Piscean Ascendant, you do things from a Capricorn motivation, but in a Piscean way, using a Piscean set of talents and abilities, and a Piscean body. The next few sections of the book explain what this means for each of the Sun/Ascendant combinations.

Some note ought to be made of the correspondence between

the Ascendant and the actual condition of the body. Since the Ascendant sign represents your physical frame rather than the personality inside it, then the appearance and well-being of that frame is also determined by the Ascendant sign. In other words, if you have a Libra Ascendant, then you should look like a Libran, and you should be subject to illnesses in the parts of the body with a special affinity to that sign.

The Astrology of Illness

This is worth a book in itself, but it is quite important to say that the astrological view of illness is that the correlation between the individual and the larger universe is maintained. In other words, if you continue over a long period of time with a way of behaviour that denies the proper and necessary expression of your planetary energies, then the organ of your body which normally handles that kind of activity for your body systems will start to show the stresses to you. A simple example: Gemini looks after the lungs, which circulate air, and from which oxygen is taken all over the body. Gemini people need to circulate among a lot of people, talking and exchanging information. They act as the lungs of society, taking news and information everywhere. They need to do this to express their planetary energies, and society needs them to do this or it is not refreshed, and does not communicate. You need your lungs to do this, too. Lungs within people, Geminis within society: same job, different levels. If you keep a Gemini, or he keeps himself, through circumstance or ignorance, in a situation where he cannot talk or circulate, or where he feels that his normal status is denied, then he is likely to develop lung trouble. This need not be anything to do with a dusty atmosphere, or whether he smokes, although obviously neither of those will help; they are external irritants, and this is an internal problem caused by imbalance in the expression of the energies built into him since birth. In the sections which follow, all the observations on health are to do with how the body shows you that certain behaviour is unbalancing you and causing unnecessary stress; problems from these causes are alleviated by listening to yourself and changing your behaviour.

Your Ascendant

Aries Ascendant

If you have Aries rising, you are an uncommon individual, because Aries only rises for about fifty minutes out of the twenty-four hour day. You must have been born around noon, or else you have got your sums wrong somewhere.

What you are trying to do with yourself is project a Capricorn personality through an Arian vehicle. You will always be trying to do things faster than anybody else, and this can lead to hastiness and a certain degree of accident-proneness. What you see as the correct way to do things involves immediate action by the most direct method, to secure instant, and measurable, results. You feel that unless you are directly and personally responsible for doing things, then they cannot be done, not only because you believe that only you can do them properly, but because you get no satisfaction from letting anybody else do anything. Personal experience of everything is the only way you learn; reading about it, or watching it, does nothing for you.

You are likely to have headaches as a recurring problem if you push yourself too hard, and you should watch your blood pressure too. Mars, ruling Aries, is a strong and forceful planet, and it is bound to get you a little over-stressed at times. You are also likely to have problems digesting things properly. Astrologically, all illnesses apply to your external condition as well as your internal condition, so think carefully; when your head aches you are banging it too hard against a problem which cannot be overcome that way, and when you are not digesting properly, you have not understood the implications of what you have taken on. In both cases, allow time to think and consider.

Taurus Ascendant

You were born at about lunchtime if you have Taurus rising. Taureans are generally fond of food—did you arrive in time for lunch, or were you a little early? You should have all the Taurean physical characteristics: quite thick-set, big around the neck and shoulders sometimes, and with large hands. You should have a broad mouth, and large eyes, which are very attractive. You should also have a good voice—not only as a singing voice, but one which is pleasant to listen to in conversation too.

The Taurean method for getting things done is to look forward to, and then enjoy, the material reward for one's efforts. It is part of Taurean thinking that if you can't touch it, buy it, own it or eat it, it isn't real and it isn't worth much. You will also be concerned to keep what is yours, not to waste your energies on what won't gain you anything or increase your possessions, and not to attempt anything which you don't think you have more than a chance of achieving.

Taureans do have taste; not only taste for food, which they love, but artistic taste, which they develop as a means of distinguishing things of value which they would then like to acquire and gain pleasure from owning. Unlike the Capricorn way of doing things, which values quality because it is valued by others, Taureans enjoy their possessions for themselves. The drawback to the Taurean approach is the lack of enterprise, and the unwillingness to try things just for the fun of it.

Taurean Ascendant people have throat and glandular problems, and all problems associated with being overweight. They can also have back and kidney problems caused as a result of an unwillingness to let things go in their external life. A lighter touch is needed in the approach to problems of possession; shedding unwanted or outworn things in a desirable process.

Gemini Ascendant

If you have a Gemini Ascendant you were born somewhere in the middle of the afternoon. You should have expressive hands and a wide range of gestures which you use as you speak (ask your friends!) and you are perhaps a little taller than average, or than other members of your family. Gemini Ascendant people also have dark hair, if there is any possibility of it in their parents' colouring, and quick, penetrating eyes which flash with amusement and mischief; Gemini Ascendant women have very fine eyes indeed.

The Gemini approach to things, which you find yourself using, is one in which the idea of a thing is seen as being the most useful, and in which no time must be lost in telling it to other people so that they can contribute their own ideas and responses to the discussion. The performance of the deed is of no real importance in the Gemini view; somebody else can do that. Ideas and their development are what you like to spend time on, and finding more people to talk to, whose ideas can be matched to your own, seems to you to offer the most satisfaction.

There are two snags to the Gemini approach. The first is that there is a surface quality to it all, in which the rough outline suffices, but no time is spent in development or long-term experience. It may seem insignificant, but there is some value in seeing a project through to the end. The second snag is similar, but is concerned with time. The Gemini approach is immediate, in that it is concerned with the present or the near future. It is difficult for a Gemini Ascendant person to see farther than a few months into the future, if that; it is even more difficult for him to extend his view sideways in time to see the impact of his actions on a wider scene. Both of these things he will dismiss as unimportant.

Gemini Ascendant people suffer from chest and lung maladies, especially when they cannot communicate what they want to or need to, or when they cannot circulate socially in the way that they would like. They also have problems eliminating wastes from their bodies, through not realizing the importance of ending things as well as beginning them. In both cases, thinking and planning on a broader scale than usual, and examination of the past to help make better use of the future, is beneficial.

Cancer Ascendant

You were born around sunset if you have your Ascendant in Cancer and your Sun in Capricorn. The Cancerian frame, through which you project your energies, may mean that you appear rounder and less lean-framed than other Capricorns.

Your energies are in no way diminished; in fact, you are likely to be even more determined to get things right. Your face could be almost cherubic, and you could have small features in a pale complexion with grey eyes and brown hair. The key to the Cancer frame is that it is paler than usual, less well defined than usual, and has no strong colouring. Strong noses and red hair do not come from a Cancerian Ascendant.

The Cancerian approach to things is highly personal. All general criticisms are taken personally, and all problems in any procedure for which they have responsibility is seen as a personal failing. You will be concerned to use your energies for the safe and secure establishment of things from the foundations up, so that you know that whatever you have been involved in has been done properly, and is unlikely to let you down in any way; you are concerned for your own safety and reputation. The other side of this approach is that you can be a little too concerned to make sure everything is done personally, and be unwilling to entrust things to other people. Not only does this overwork you, it seems obsessive and uncooperative to others.

The Cancer Ascendant person has health problems with the maintenance of the flow of fluids in his body, and a tendency to stomach ulcers caused by worry. Cancer Ascendant women should pay special attention to their breasts, since the affinity between the sign, the Moon as ruler of all things feminine, and that particular body system means that major imbalances in the life are likely to show there first. There could also be some problems with the liver and the circulation of the legs; the answer is to think that, metaphorically, you do not have to support everybody you know: they can use their own legs to stand on, and you do not have to feed them either.

Leo Ascendant

You were born in the early evening if you have Leo as an Ascendant. Leo, as the determinant of the physical characteristics, makes itself known by the lion of the sign—you can always spot the deep chest, proud and slightly pompous way of walking, and, more often than not, the hair arranged in some sort of a mane, either full or taken back off the face, and golden if possible. Leo Ascendant people have strong voices and a definite presence to them. A Leo Ascendant will bring to the fore any hereditary tendency to golden colouring, so reddish or golden hair, or a rosy complexion may be in evidence, as will a heavy build in the upper half of the body .

The Leonine way of doing things is to put yourself in the centre and work from the centre outwards, making sure that everybody knows where the commands are coming from. It is quite a tiring way of working; you need to put a lot of energy into it, because you are acting as the driving force for everybody else. Preferred situations for this technique are those where you already know, more or less, what's going to happen; this way you are unlikely to be thrown off balance by unexpected developments. The grand gesture belongs to the Leo method; it works best if all processes are converted into theatrical scenes, with roles acted rather than lived. Over-reaction, over-dramatization, and over-indulgence are common, but the approach is in essence kind-hearted and well-meant. Children enjoy being with Leo Ascendant people, and they enjoy having children around them. The flaws in the approach are only that little gets done in difficult circumstances where applause and appreciation are scarce commodities, and that little is attempted that is really new and innovatory.

The health problems of the Leo Ascendant person come from the heart, and also from the joints, which suffer from mobility problems. These both come from a lifetime of being at the centre of things and working for everybody's good, and from being too stiff and unwilling to try any change in position. The remedy, of course, is to be more flexible, and to allow your friends to repay the favours they owe you.

Virgo Ascendant

A birth in the late evening puts Virgo on the Ascendant. Physically, this should make you slim and rather long, especially in the body; even if you have broad shoulders you will still have a long waist. There is a neatness to the features, but nothing notable; hair is brown, but again nothing notable. The nose and chin are often well-defined, and the forehead is often both tall and broad; the voice can be a little shrill and lacks penetration.

The Virgoan Ascendant person does not have an approach to life; he has a *system*. He analyses everything and pays a lot of attention to the way in which he works. It is important to the person with Virgo rising not only to be effective, but to be efficient; you can always interest them in a new or better technique. They watch themselves work, as if from a distance, all the while wondering if they can do it better. They never mind repetition; in fact they quite enjoy it, because as they get more proficient they feel better about things. To you, being able to do things is everything, and unless you are given a practical outlet for your energies, you are completely ineffective. There is a willingness to help others, to be of service through being able to offer a superior technique, inherent in the Virgo way of doing things, which prevents Virgo rising people from being seen as cold and unfriendly. They appreciate their help being appreciated. The problems in the Virgo attitude are a tendency to go into things in more detail than is necessary, and to be too much concerned with the 'proper' way to do things.

People with a Virgo Ascendant are susceptible to intestinal problems, and also circulatory problems, and maybe poor sight. All of these are ways in which the body registers the stresses of being too concerned with digesting the minutiae of things which are meant to be passed through anyway, and by not getting enough social contact. The remedy is to lift your head from your workbench sometimes, admit that the act is sometimes more important than the manner of its performance, and not to take things too seriously.

Libra Ascendant

You were born around midnight if you have Libra rising; it will give you a pleasant and approachable manner which will do a great deal to hide your anxieties and prevent people thinking anything but the best of you. You should be tallish, and graceful, as all Libra Ascendant people tend to be; they have a clear complexion, and blue eyes if possible, set in an oval face with finely formed features.

The Libra Ascendant person has to go through life at a fairly relaxed pace. The sign that controls his body won't let him feel rushed or anxious; if that sort of thing looks likely, then he will slow down a little until the panic's over. There is a need to see yourself reflected in the eyes of others, and so you will form a large circle of friends. You define your own opinion of yourself through their responses to you, rather than being sure what you want, and not caring what they think.

The drawback to the Libran approach is that unless you have approval from others, you are unlikely to do anything on your own initiative, or at least you find it hard to decide on a course of action. You always want to do things in the way which will cause the least bother to anyone, and to produce an acceptable overall result; sometimes this isn't definite enough, and you need to know what you do want as well as what you don't.

The Libran Ascendant makes the body susceptible to all ailments of the kidneys and of the skin; there may also be trouble in the feet. The kidney ailments are from trying to take all the problems out of life as you go along. Sometimes it's better simply to attack a few of the obstacles and knock them flat in pure rage—and in doing so you will develop adrenaline from the adrenal glands, on top of the kidneys!

Scorpio Ascendant

You were born in the small hours of the morning if you have a Scorpio Ascendant. A Scorpio Ascendant should give you a dark and powerful look, with a solid build, though not necessarily over-muscled, Scorpio Ascendant people tend to have a very penetrating and level way of looking at others, which is often disconcerting. Any possible darkness in the colouring is usually displayed, with dark complexions and dark hair, often thick and curly, never fine.

The Scorpio Ascendant person usually does things in a controlled manner. He is not given to explosive releases of energy unless they are absolutely necessary; even then, not often. He knows, or feels (a better word, since the Scorpionic mind makes decisions as a result of knowledge gained by feeling rather than thinking), that he has plenty of energy to spare, but uses it in small and effective doses, each one suited to the requirements of the task at hand. It does not seem useful to him to put in more effort than is strictly necessary for any one activity; that extra energy could be used somewhere else. The idea that overdoing things for their own sake is sometimes fun because of the sheer exhilaration of the release of energy does not strike a responsive chord in the Scorpio body, nor even much understanding. There is, however, understanding and perception of a situation which exists at more than one level. If anything is complicated, involving many activities and many people, with much interaction and many side issues which must be considered, then the Scorpio Ascendant person sees it all and understands all of it, in its minutest detail. They feel, and understand, the responses from all of their surroundings at once, but do not necessarily feel involved with them unless they choose to make a move. When they do move, they will have the intention of transforming things, making them different to conform to their ideas of how things need to be arranged.

Scorpio Ascendant people are unable simply to possess and look after anything; they must change it and direct it their way, and this can be a disadvantage.

Scorpio illnesses are usually to do with the genital and excretory systems; problems here relate to a lifestyle in which things are thrown away when used, or sometimes rejected when there is still use in them. It may be that there is too much stress on being the founder of the new, and on organizing others; this will bring head pains, and illnesses of that order. The solution is to take on the existing situation as it is, and look after it without changing any of it.

Sagittarius Ascendant

It would have been just before breakfast when you were born for you to have a Sagittarius Ascendant. If you have, you should be taller than average, with a sort of sporty, leggy look to you; you should have a long face with pronounced temples (you may be balding there if you are male), a well-coloured complexion, clear eyes, and brown hair. A Grecian nose is sometimes a feature of this physique.

The Sagittarian Ascendant gives a way of working that is based on mobility and change. This particular frame can't keep still and is much more comfortable walking than standing, more comfortable lounging or leaning than sitting formally. You tend to be in a bit of a hurry; travelling takes up a lot of your time, because you enjoy it so. It is probably true to say that you enjoy the process of driving more than whatever it is that you have to do when you get there. You probably think a lot of your car, and you are likely to have one which is more than just a machine for transport—you see it as an extension, a representation even, of yourself. People will notice how outgoing and friendly you seem to be, but they will need to know you for some time before they realize that you enjoy meeting people more than almost anything else, and you dislike being with the same companions all the time. There is a constant restlessness in you; you will feel that being static is somehow unnatural, and it worries you. You are an optimist, but can also be an opportunist, in that you see no reason to stay doing one thing for a moment longer than it interests you. The inability to stay and develop a situation or give long-term commitment to anything is the biggest failing of this sign's influence.

A person with Sagittarius rising can expect to have problems with his hips and thighs, and possibly in his arterial system; this is to do with trying to leap too far at once, in all senses. You may also have liver and digestive problems, again caused by haste on a long-term scale. The remedy is to shorten your horizons and concentrate on things nearer home.

Capricorn Ascendant

It must have been around sunrise when you were born for you to have a Capricorn Ascendant. This sign often gives a small frame, quite compact and built to last a long time, the sort that doesn't need a lot of feeding and isn't big enough or heavy enough to break when it falls over. The face can be narrow and the features small; often the mouth points downwards at the corners, and this doesn't change even when the person smiles or laughs.

The Capricorn sees life as an ordered, dutiful struggle. There is a great deal of emphasis placed on projecting and maintaining appearances, both in the professional and the personal life; the idea of 'good reputation' is one which everybody with Capricorn rising, whatever their sun sign, recognizes at once. There is a sense of duty and commitment which the Sagittarian Ascendant simply cannot understand; here the feeling is that there are things which need doing, so you just have to set to and get them done. Capricorn Ascendant people see far forwards in time, anticipating their responsibilities for years to come, even if their Sun sign does not normally function this way; in such cases they apply themselves to one problem at a time, but can envisage a succession of problems, one after another, going on for years.

The disadvantages of this outlook are to do with its static nature. There is often a sense of caution that borders on the paranoid, and while this is often well disguised in affluent middle-class middle age, it seems a little odd in the young. This tends to make for a critical assessment of all aspects of a new venture before embarking on it and as a result a lot of the original impetus is lost. This makes the result less than was originally hoped in many cases, and so a cycle of disappointment and unadventurousness sets in, which is difficult to break. The Capricorn Ascendant person is often humourless, and can seem determined to remain so.

These people have trouble in their joints, and break bones from time to time, entirely as a result of being inflexible. On a small scale this can be from landing badly in an accident because the Capricorn Ascendant keeps up appearances to the very end, refusing to believe that an accident could be happening to him: on a large scale, a refusal to move with the times can lead to the collapse of an outmoded set of values when they are swept away by progress, and this breaking up of an old structure can also cripple. They can get lung troubles, too, as a result of not taking enough fresh air, or fresh ideas. The best treatment is to look after their families rather than their reputation, and to think about the difference between stability and stagnation.

Aquarius Ascendant

Having an Aquarius Ascendant means that you were born in the middle of the morning. This will make you more sociable than you would otherwise have been, with a strong interest in verbal communication. An Aquarian Ascendant will also make

There is a certain clarity, not to say transparency, about the Aquarian physique. It is usually tall, fair, and well shaped, almost never small or dark. There is nothing about the face which is particularly distinctive; no noticeable colouring, shape of nose, brows, or any other feature. It is an average sort of face, cleanly formed and clear.

The person with an Aquarian Ascendant wants to be independent. Not violently so, not the sort of independence that fights its way out of wherever it feels it's been put, just different from everybody else. Aquarius gives your body the ability to do things in ways perhaps not done before; you can discover new techniques and practices for yourself and don't need to stay in the ways you were taught. There is a willingness to branch out, to try new things; not a Scorpionic wish to make things happen the way you want, but an amused curiosity which would just like to see if things are any better done a different way. There is no need for you to convince the world that your way is best: it only needs to suit you.

Of course, an Aquarian needs to measure his difference against others, and therefore you feel better when you have a few friends around you to bounce ideas off, as well as showing them how you're doing things in a slightly different way. You function best in groups, and feel physically at ease when you're not the only person in the room. You are not necessarily the leader of the group; just a group member. Group leaders put their energy into the group, and you draw strength and support from it, so you are unlikely to be the leader, though paradoxically all groups work better for having you in them.

A handicap arising from an Aquarian Ascendant is that you

are unlikely to really feel passionately involved with anything, and this may mean that unless you have support from your friends and colleagues you will be unable to muster the determination necessary to overcome really sizeable obstacles in your chosen career.

You are likely to suffer from diseases of the circulation and in your lower legs and ankles; these may reflect a life where too much time is spent trying to be independent, and not enough support is sought from others. You may also get stomach disorders and colds because you are not generating enough heat: get more involved in things and angrier about them!

Pisces Ascendant

You were born in the late morning if you have Pisces rising. Like Aries rising, Pisces is only possible as an Ascendant for about fifty minutes, so there aren't many of you around. A Piscean Ascendant will also make for great success in your chosen career. No matter what the job is, being born around the middle of the day guarantees public prominence whether you want it or not.

Pisces Ascendant people are on the small side, with a tendency to be a bit pale and fleshy. They are not very well coordinated and so walk rather clumsily, despite the fact that their feet are often large. They have large, expressive, but rather sleepy-looking eyes.

As a Capricorn with Pisces rising, you will prefer to let things come to you than go out and look for them; it will seem a lot safer that way to you. Safety will be a prime consideration of yours; your natural Capricornian caution will blend with the evasiveness of the Piscean to produce a habit of always making sure that you have your escape route organized in case anything should go wrong. Pisces will help you think and consider things in ways which are closed to other Capricorns—your imagination will be a lot more active, for a start, and you will be able to spot those odd times when you find yourself being guided by motives which are other than coldly logical. You will still be out to improve your station in life, but you will be more considerate, and more compassionate, than other Capricorns.

The major problem with a Pisces Ascendant is this inability to be active rather than reactive; you would rather be reacting to outside influences than generating your own movements from within yourself.

A Piscean Ascendant gives problems with the feet and the lymphatic system; this has connections with the way you move in response to external pressures, and how you deal with things which invade your system from outside. You may also suffer from faint-heartedness—literally as well as metaphorically. The remedy is to be more definite and less influenced by opinions other than your own.

6. Three Crosses: Areas of Life that Affect Each Other

If you have already determined your Ascendant sign from page 74, and you have read 'The Meaning of the Zodiac' on page 11, you can apply that knowledge to every area of your life with revealing results. Instead of just looking at yourself, you can see how things like your career and your finances work from the unique point of view of your birth moment.

You will remember how the Ascendant defined which way up the sky was. Once you have it the right way up, then you can divide it into sectors for different areas of life, and see which zodiac signs occupy them. After that, you can interpret each sector of sky in the light of what you know about the zodiac sign which fell in it at the time that you were born.

Below there is a circular diagram of the sky, with the horizon splitting it across the middle. This is the way real horoscopes are usually drawn. In the outer circle, in the space indicated, write the name of your Ascendant sign, not your Sun sign (unless they are the same, of course. If you don't know your time of birth, and so can't work out an Ascendant, use your Sun sign.) Make it overlap sectors 12 and 1, so that the degree of your Ascendant within that sign is on the eastern horizon. Now fill in the rest of the zodiac around the circle in sequence, one across each sector boundary. If you've forgotten the sequence, look at the diagram on page 16. When you've done that, draw a symbol for the Sun (☉—a circle with a point at its centre) in one of the sectors which has your Sun sign at its edge. Think about how far through the sign your Sun is; make sure that you have put it in the right sector. Whichever sector this is will be very important to you; having the Sun there gives a bias to the whole chart, like the weight on one side of a locomotive wheel. You will feel that the activities of that sector (or house, as they are usually called) are most in keeping with your character, and you feel comfortable doing that sort of thing.

Make sure you have got your sums right. As a Sagittarius born in the afternoon, you might well have Taurus rising, and the Sun in the eighth house, for example.

Now is the time to examine the twelve numbered sections of your own sky, and see what there is to be found.

Angular Houses: 1, 4, 7, 10

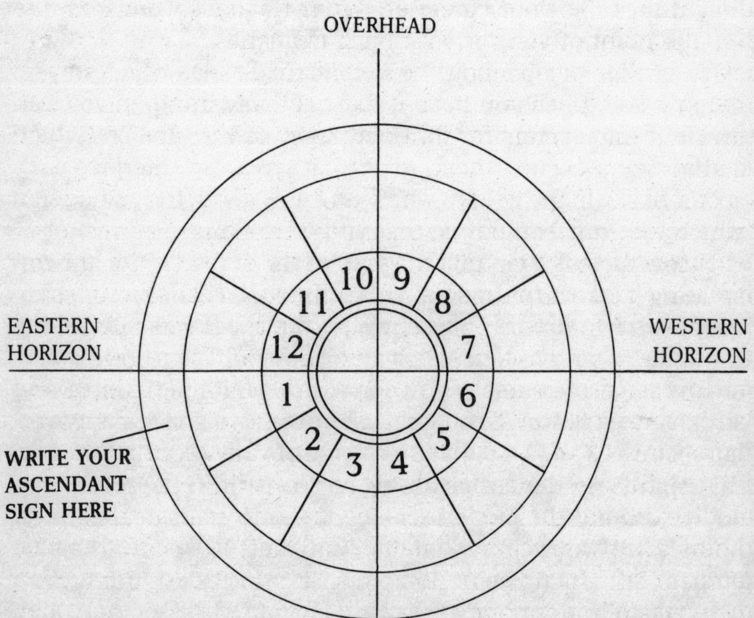

These are the houses closest to the horizon and the vertical, reading round in zodiacal sequence. The first house is concerned with you yourself as a physical entity, your appearance, and your health. Most of this has been dealt with in the section on Ascendants. If you have the Sun here, it simply doubles the impact of your Sun sign energies.

Opposite to you is the seventh house, which concerns itself with everybody who is not you. Partners in a business sense, husbands, wives, enemies you are actually aware of (and who therefore stand opposed to you in plain sight) and any other unclassified strangers all belong in the seventh house. You see their motivation as being of the opposite sign to your Ascendant sign, as being something you are not. If you have Capricorn rising, you see them as behaving, and needing to be treated, which is perhaps more accurate, in a Cancerian manner. This is how you approach seventh-house things. Use the keywords from 'The Meaning of the Zodiac' (p. 17) to remind yourself what this is. If you have the Sun in the seventh house you are your own best partner: you may marry late in life, or not at all. Perhaps your marriage will be unsuccessful. It is not a failure; it is simply that you are to a very great extent self-supporting, and have neither the ability nor the need to share yourself completely with another.

The whole business of the first and the seventh is to do with 'me and not-me'. For the personal energies of this relationship to be shown in tangible form, it is necessary to look at the pair of houses whose axis most squarely crosses the first/seventh axis. This is the fourth/tenth. The tenth is your received status in the world, and is the actual answer to the question 'What do you take me for?' No matter what you do, the world will find it best to see you as doing the sort of thing shown by the sign at the start of the tenth house. Eventually, you will start to pursue that kind of activity anyway, because in doing so you get more appreciation and reward from the rest of society. Your efforts in dealing with others, which is a first/seventh thing, have their result in the tenth, and their origins in the fourth. Expect to find clues there to your family, your home, the beliefs you hold most dear, and the eventual conclusion to your life (not your death, which is a different matter). If you have the Sun in the tenth, you will achieve some measure of prominence or fame; if your sun is in the fourth, you will do well in property, and your family will be of greater importance to you than is usual.

There is, of course, some give and take between the paired houses. Giving more time to yourself in the first house means that you are denying attention to the seventh, your partner; the reverse also applies. Giving a lot of attention to your career, in the tenth house, stops you from spending quite so much time as you might like with your family or at home. Spending too much time at home means that you are out of the public eye. There is only so much time in a day; what you give to one must be denied to the other.

This cross of four houses defines most people's lives: self, partner, home, and career. An over-emphasis on any of these is to the detriment of the other three, and all the arms of the cross feel and react to any event affecting any single member.

If these four houses have cardinal signs on them in your chart, then you are very much the sort of person who feels that he is in control of his own life, and that it is his duty to shape it into something new, personal, and original. You feel that by making decisive moves with your own circumstances you can actually change the way your life unfolds, and enjoy steering it the way you want it to go.

If these four houses have fixed signs on them in your chart, then you are the sort of person who sees the essential shape of your life as being one of looking after what you were given, continuing in the tradition, and ending up with a profit at the end of it all. Like a farmer, you see yourself as a tenant of the land you inherited, with a responsibility to hand it on in at least as good a condition as it was when you took it over. You are likely to see the main goal in all life's ups and downs as the maintenance of stability and enrichment of what you possess.

If these four houses have mutable signs on them in your chart, then you are much more willing to change yourself to suit circumstances than the other two. Rather than seeing yourself as the captain of your ship, or the trustee of the family firm, you see yourself as free to adapt to challenges as they arise, and if necessary to make fundamental changes in your life, home and career to suit the needs of the moment. You are the sort to welcome change and novelty, and you don't expect to have anything to show for it at the end of the day except experience. There is a strong sense of service in the mutable signs, and if you spend your life working for the welfare of others, then they will have something to show for it while you will not. Not in physical terms, anyway; you will have had your reward by seeing your own energies transformed into their success.

The Succedent Houses: 2, 5, 8, 11

These houses are called succedent because they succeed, or follow on from, the previous four. Where the angular houses define the framework of the life, the succedent ones give substance, and help develop it to its fullest and richest extent, in exactly the same way as fixed signs show the development and maintenance of the elemental energies defined by the cardinal signs.

The second house and the eighth define your resources; how much you have to play with, so to speak. The fifth and eleventh show what you do with it, and how much you achieve. Your immediate environment is the business of the second house. Your tastes in furniture and clothes are here (all part of your immediate environment, if you think about it) as well as your immediate resources, food and cash. Food is a resource because without it you are short of energy, and cash is a resource for obvious reasons. If you have the Sun here you are likely to be fond of spending money, and fond of eating too! You are likely to place value on things that you can buy or possess, and judge your success by your bank balance.

Opposed to it, and therefore dealing with the opposite viewpoint, is the eighth house, where you will find stored money. Savings, bank accounts, mortgages, and all kinds of non-immediate money come under this house. So do major and irreversible changes in your life, because they are the larger environment rather than the immediate one. Surgical operations and death are both in the eighth, because you are not the same person afterwards, and that is an irreversible change. If you have the Sun in the eighth you are likely to be very careful with yourself, and not the sort to expose yourself to any risk; you are also not likely to be short of a few thousand when life gets tight, because eighth house people always have some extra resource tucked away somewhere. You are also likely to benefit from legacies, which are another form of long-term wealth.

To turn all this money into some form of visible wealth you must obviously do something with it, and all forms of self-expression and ambition are found in the fifth and the eleventh houses. The fifth is where you have fun, basically; all that you like to do, all that amuses you, all your hobbies are found there, and a look at the zodiac sign falling in that house in your chart will show you what it is that you like so much. Your children are a fifth-house phenomenon, too; they are an expression of yourself made physical, made from the substance of your body and existence, and given their own. If you have the Sun in the fifth house you are likely to be of a generally happy disposition, confident that life is there to be enjoyed, and sure that something good will turn up.

The eleventh house, in contrast, is not so much what you like doing as what you would like to be doing: it deals with hopes, wishes, and ambitions. It also deals with friends and all social gatherings, because in a similar manner to the Aries/Libra axis, anybody who is 'not-you' and enjoying themselves must be opposed to you enjoying yourself in the fifth house. If you have the Sun in the eleventh house, you are at your best in a group. You would do well in large organizations, possibly political ones, and will find that you can organize well. You have well-defined ambitions, and know how to realize them, using other people as supporters of your cause.

The oppositions in this cross work just as effectively as the previous set did: cash is either used or stored, and to convert it from one to the other diminishes the first. Similarly, time spent enjoying yourself does nothing for your ambitions and aims, nor does it help you maintain relationships with all the groups of people you know; there again, all work and no play . . .

If you have cardinal signs on these four houses in your chart, then you think that using all the resources available to you at any one time is important. Although what you do isn't necessarily important, or even stable, you want to have something to show for it, and enjoying yourself as you go along is important to you. To you, money is for spending, and how your friends see you is To you, money is for spending, and how your friends see you is possibly more important to you than how you see yourself.

Fixed signs on these four houses will make you reticent, and careful of how you express yourself. You are possibly too busy with the important things of life as you see them, such as your career and long-term prospects, to give much attention to the way you live. You feel it is important to have things of quality, because you have a long-term view of life, and you feel secure when you have some money in the bank, but you don't enjoy your possessions and friends for your own sake. You have them because you feel that you should, not because they are reason enough in themselves.

Mutable signs on these four houses show a flexible attitude to the use of a resource, possibly because the angular houses show that you already have plenty of it, and it is your duty to use it well. You don't mind spending time and money on projects which to you are necessary, and which will have a measurable end result. You see that you need to spend time and effort to bring projects into a completed reality, and you are willing to do that as long as the final product is yours and worth having. You are likely to change your style of living quite frequently during your life, and there may be ambitions which, when fulfilled, fade from your life completely.

The Cadent Houses: 3, 6, 9, 12

The final four houses are called cadent either because they fall away from the angles (horizon and vertical axes), or because they

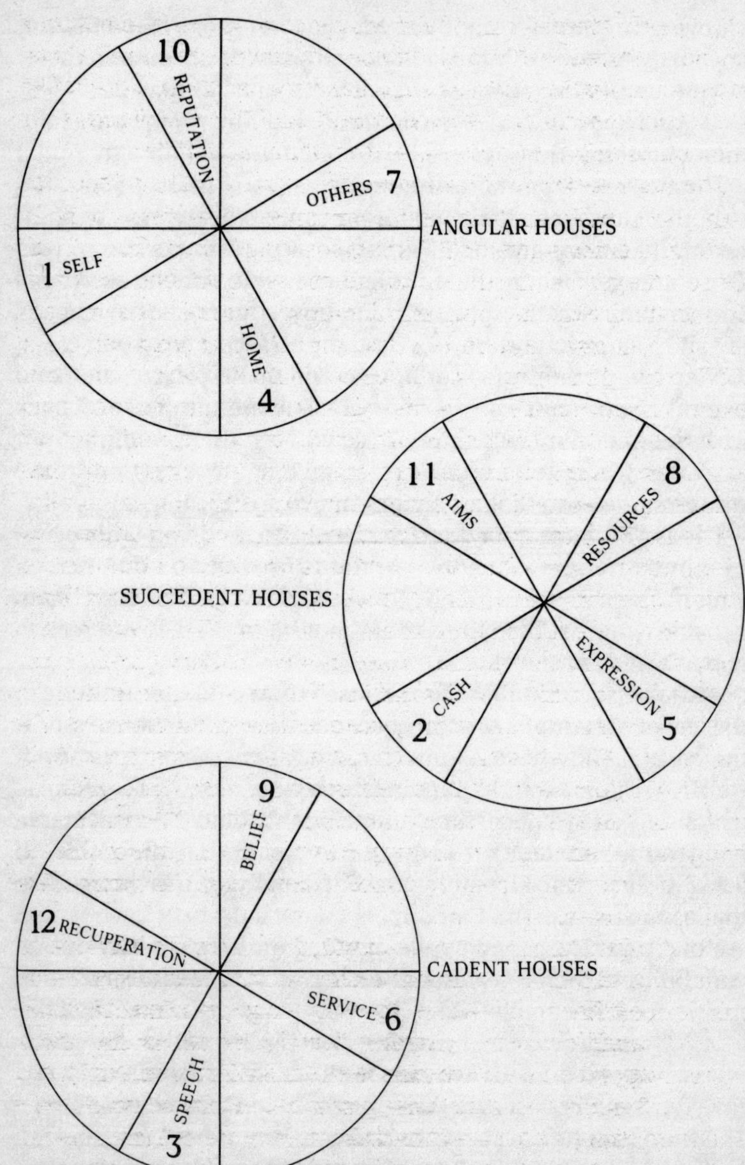
10
REPUTATION
OTHERS 7
ANGULAR HOUSES
1 SELF
HOME
4
11
AIMS
8
RESOURCES
SUCCEDENT HOUSES
EXPRESSION
CASH
2
5
9
BELIEF
12 RECUPERATION
CADENT HOUSES
SERVICE 6
SPEECH
3

fall towards them, giving their energy towards the formation of the next phase in their existence. Either way, affairs in these houses are nothing like as firm and active as those in the other two sets of four. It may be useful to think of them as being given to mental rather than physical or material activities.

The third and ninth houses are given to thought and speech, with the ninth specializing in incoming thoughts, such as reading, learning and belief (religions of all kinds are ninth-house things), while the third limits itself to speaking and writing, daily chat, and the sort of conversations you have every day. If you have the Sun in the third house, you will be a chatterbox. Talking is something you could do all day, and you love reading. Anything will do—papers, magazines, novels; as long as it has words in it you will like it. You will have the sort of mind that loves accumulating trivia, but you may find that serious study or hard learning is something that you cannot do.

The third house concerns itself with daily conversation, but the ninth is more withdrawn. Study is easy for a ninth-house person, but since all ideal and theoretical thought belongs here, the down-to-earth street-corner reality of the third house doesn't, and so the higher knowledge of the ninth finds no application in daily life. The third-ninth axis is the difference between practical street experience and the refined learning of a university. To give time to one must mean taking time from the other. If you have the Sun in the ninth, you are likely to have a very sure grasp of the theory of things, and could well be an instigator or director of large projects; but you are unable to actually do the things yourself. Knowledge is yours, but application is not.

How this knowledge gets applied in the production of something new is a matter of technique, and technique is the business of the sixth house. The way things get done, both for yourself and for other people's benefit, is all in the sixth. Everything you do on someone else's behalf is there, too. If you have the Sun in the sixth house, you are careful and considerate by nature, much concerned to make the best use of things and to do things in the best way possible. Pride of work and craftsmanship are guiding words to you; any kind of sloppiness is upsetting. You look after yourself, too; health is a sixth-house thing, and the Sun in the sixth sometimes makes you something of a hypochondriac.

Opposed to the sixth, and therefore opposed to the ideas of doing things for others, mastering the proper technique, and looking after your physical health, is the twelfth house. This is concerned with withdrawing yourself from the world, being on your own, having time to think. Energy is applied to the job in hand in the sixth house, and here it is allowed to grow again without being applied to anything. Recuperation is a good word to remember. All forms of rest are twelfth-house concepts. If you have the Sun in the twelfth house you are an essentially private individual, and there will be times when you need to be on your own to think about things and recover your strength and balance. You will keep your opinions to yourself, and share very little of your emotional troubles with anyone. Yours is most definitely not a life lived out in the open.

These houses live in the shadow of the houses which follow them. Each of them is a preparation for the next phase. If your Sun is in any of these houses, your life is much more one of giving away than of accumulation. You already have the experience and the knowledge, and you will be trying to hand it on before you go, so to speak. Acquisition is something you will never manage on a permanent basis.

If these houses have Cardinal signs on them in your chart, then preparation for things to come is important to you, and you think in straight lines towards a recognized goal. You will have firm and rather simplistic views and beliefs about matters which are not usually described in such terms, such as morality and politics, and you will be used to saying things simply and with meaning. Deception and half-truths, even mild exaggeration, confuse you, because you do not think in that sort of way.

If fixed signs occupy these houses in your horoscope, your thinking is conservative, and your mind, though rich and varied in its imagination, is not truly original. You like to collect ideas from elsewhere and tell yourself that they are your own. You rely on changing circumstances to bring you variety, and your own beliefs and opinions stay fixed to anchor you in a changing world; unfortunately, this can mean a refusal to take in new ideas, shown in your behaviour as a rather appealing old-fashionedness.

Having mutable signs on these houses in your horoscope shows a flexible imagination, though often not a very practical one. Speech and ideas flow freely from you, and you are quick to adapt your ideas to suit the occasion, performing complete changes of viewpoint without effort if required. You seem to have grasped the instinctive truth that mental images and words are not real, and can be changed or erased at will; you are far less inhibited in their use than the other two groups, who regard words as something at least as heavy as cement, and nearly as difficult to dissolve. Periods in the public eye and periods of isolation are of equal value to you; you can use them each for their best purpose, and have no dislike of either. This great flexibility of mind does mean, though, that you lack seriousness of approach at times, and have a happy-go-lucky view of the future, and of things spiritual, which may lead to eventual disappointments and regrets.

Houses are important in a horoscope. The twelve sectors of the sky correspond to the twelve signs of the zodiac, the difference being that the zodiac is a product of the Sun's annual revolution, and the houses are a product (via the Ascendant) of the Earth's daily revolution. They bring the symbolism down one level from the sky to the individual, and they answer the questions which arise when people of the same Sun sign have different lives and different preferences. The house in which the Sun falls, and the qualities of the signs in the houses, show each person's approach to those areas of his life, and the one which will be the most important to him.

Part 4
Capricorn Trivia

7. Tastes and Preferences

Clothes

There are two sorts of Capricorns—the super-smart high-profile fashion plate sort, and the total scruff. You will know which one you are: if you don't, ask your friends!

Capricorn, as we have noted before, is the sign concerned with the skin and the bones. This is because Saturn represents the outer limits of the universe, and its underlying structure. Your clothes are the outer limit of your body; they replace your skin, in that they are what people see of you. Therefore you are concerned to show that you are given the recognition you deserve for your position in life through that Capricornian outer layer—your clothes. In other words, you want to show your status through what you wear. If you are one of the scruffy Capricorns, it is probably because you are working so hard that you haven't given yourself time to consider this aspect of yourself, and you are probably overworking if that is the case.

Whatever you wear, it will reflect the influence of Saturn. That means that you will choose things in serious colours, such as greys and blacks. It also means that you will have a liking for heavy fabrics; lightweight stuff suggests flimsiness and lack of substance, which is not the sort of thing you want to be associated with at all. Finally, it means that you will choose traditional and conservative styles: not only does Capricorn like things which have stood the test of time, it also likes to show power and authority, and that is usually expressed through conservative but expensive taste.

Capricorn and money go together, and you are likely to look for ways to show your money through your clothes. Traditionally this has been done throughout history by the use of luxury fabrics—medieval noblemen didn't wear fur round their cloaks just to keep warm, they did it to show how wealthy and powerful they were, too. The twentieth-century equivalent, at least for Capricorn women, is a mink coat.

Leather is actually a Capricornian fabric, despite every astrology book you have ever read insisting that it is Scorpionic. The reason is simple: it is strong, it is long-lasting, and when all's said and done, it's *skin*!

Capricorn men wear suits to work; some of them wear suits on their days off, too. The suit is the Capricorn garment *par excellence*; it is formal, it is standardized, it shows that you mean business, and it has a tradition behind it. Capricorn women have always liked suits, too: they have made quite a comeback in recent years, largely due to the influence of the planet Neptune, influencing society as a whole, which is currently in Capricorn. Whatever else they wear, Capricorn women wait for a style to become established before they wear it; they are not great experimenters. This is because you cannot increase your reputation by wearing something too new for society to have an opinion on.

Finally, the Capricorn's liking for hard, Saturnine fabrics and the extra skin of leather extends to the extremities of his body. Capricorn women love wearing high boots; it's not because they are trying to look sexy, but because they are trying to look powerful and elegant at the same time. They enjoy wearing gloves, too, for similar reasons.

Food and Furnishings

A Capricorn's taste in food is very traditional. He eats the things that he has always eaten, and is particularly fond of any recipes which have been handed down in his family, because his sense of history and continuity add to his enjoyment of the dish itself. Despite the fact that he is likely, at least in later life, to be reasonably affluent, he isn't too keen on luxury foods; Capricorns are rather sparing in their treatment of themselves, and they see no reason why they should eat rich and rare delicacies when simpler food is just as nourishing. Sometimes this is taken to extremes, as in the cases which crop up from time to time of misers who starve themselves to death.

Capricorn houses are often impressive. It is true that the sort of Capricorn whose cares sit too heavily on him—the scruffy, careworn, undernourished sort—often has a home which seems empty of comforts and luxuries, but the rest of the sign does all that it can to make its home an advertisement for its status. Capricorns aren't fond of houses because they are family homes; they are fond of them because they are solid, lasting, impressive, and an appreciating asset.

Inside, they are furnished in a traditional style, but in the very finest quality materials. The overall purpose is for the visitor to wonder how much it must all have cost. Status symbols are all over the place. Although a lot of time and effort has been lavished on the place, unless there is the influence of another, non-Capricorn person around to add warmth and balance, the overall effect can be rather forbidding and cold.

Hobbies

Capricorns work too hard and for too long to have any time for hobbies and recreation. When their doctors tell them to relax, though, they go out and do the sort of sports you would expect a Goat to do: walking in the hills, climbing, that sort of thing. The emphasis all the time is on cold, hard sports involving cold, hard rocks, suitable for a mixture of Saturn and an Earth sign.

When they stay indoors, they read history books. Biographies of famous people from the past appeal to Capricorns particularly—their sense of time helps them look at a whole life at once, and their sense of tradition and history helps them feel at home in the past.

8. Capricorn Luck

Being lucky isn't a matter of pure luck. It can be engineered. What happens when you are lucky is that a number of correspondences are made between circumstances, people, and even material items, which eventually enable planetary energies to flow quickly and effectively to act with full force in a particular way. If you are part of that chain, or your intentions lie in the same direction as the planetary flow, then you say that things are going your way, or that you are lucky. All you have to do to maximize this tendency is to make sure you are aligned to the flow of energies from the planets whenever you want things to work your way.

It is regular astrological practice to try to reinforce your own position in these things, by attracting energies which are already strongly represented in you. For a Capricorn, this means Saturn, of course, and therefore any 'lucky' number, colour, or whatever for a Capricorn is simply going to be one of those which correspond symbolically to the attributes of Saturn.

Saturn's colour is black; therefore a Capricorn's lucky colour is black, because by wearing it or aligning himself to it, for example by betting on a horse whose jockey's silks are black, or supporting a sporting team whose colours include black, he aligns himself to the energies of Saturn, and thereby recharges the solar energies that are already in him.

A Capricorn's preferred gemstone is an onyx; moonstone is

sometimes quoted too. Gemstones are seen as being able to concentrate or focus magical energies, and the colour of the stone shows its propensity to the energies of a particular planet. There are other stones quoted for the sign, such as jet; in most cases it is the colour which is the key.

Because Capricorn is the tenth sign, your lucky number is 10. Saturn has its own number, which is 4 (though some authorities quote 3); that will be lucky for you too, and all combinations of numbers which add up to 4 by reduction work the same way, so you have a range to choose from. Reducing a number is done by adding its digits until you can go no further. As an example, take 472, $4+7+2=13$, and then $1+3=4$. There you are—472 is a lucky number for you, so to buy a car with those digits in its registration plate would make it a car which, while you had it, you were very fond of, and which served you well.

Saturn also has its own day, Saturday (Saturn's day, yes?), and Capricorn has a direction with which it is associated, the South. If you have something important to do, and you manage to put it into action on Saturday 4th October (month number 10, remember), then you will have made sure that you will get the result best suited to you, by aligning yourself to your own planet and helping its energies flow through you and your activity unimpeded.

Saturn also has a metal associated with it, and in the Middle Ages people wore jewellery made of their planetary metals for luck, or self-alignment and emphasis, whichever way you want to describe it. In the case of Capricorn and Saturn, that metal is lead. I know you are not likely to wear jewellery made of lead, but these days Capricorns have something else to fulfil the purpose: they have heavy and imposing cars which enclose them in a Saturnine manner and are often in Capricorn colours. If you can't see a black BMW as Capricorn jewellery then you have no imagination!

There are plants and herbs for each planet, and foods too. Among Saturn's plants are mandrake and deadly nightshade, the vegetables spinach and parsnip, and the herb sage.

There is almost no end to the list of correspondences between the planets and everyday items, and many more can be made if you have a good imagination. They are lucky for Capricorns if you know what makes them so, and if you believe them to be so; the essence of the process lies in linking yourself and the object of your intent with some identifiable token of your own planet, such as its colour or number, and strengthening yourself thereby. The stronger you are, then the more frequently you will be able to achieve the result you want—and that's all that luck is, isn't it?

A Final Word

By the time you reach here, you will have learnt a great deal more about yourself. At least, I hope you have.

You will probably have noticed that I appear to have contradicted myself in some parts of the book, and repeated myself in others, and there are reasons for this. It is quite likely that I have said that your Sun position makes you one way, while your Ascendant makes you the opposite. There is nothing strange about this; nobody is consistent, the same the whole way through—everybody has contradictory sides to their character, and knowing some more about your Sun sign and your Ascendant will help you to label and define those contradictory elements. It won't do anything about dealing with them, though—that's your job, and always has been. The only person who can live your horoscope is you. Astrology won't make your problems disappear, and it never has been able to; it simply defines the problems more clearly, and enables you to look for answers.

Where I have repeated myself it is either to make the point for the benefit of the person who is only going to read that section of the book, or because you have a double helping of the energy of your sign, as in the instance of the Sun and Ascendant in the same sign.

I hope you found the relationships section useful; you may well find that the Sun-to-Ascendant comparison is just as useful in showing you how you fit in with your partner as the usual Sun-to-Sun practice.

Where do you go from here? If you want to learn more about astrology, and see how all of the planets fit into the picture of the sky as it was at your birth, then you must either consult an astrologer or learn how to do it for yourself. There is quite a lot of astrology around these days; evening classes are not too hard to find and there are groups of enthusiasts up and down the country. There are also plenty of books which will show you how to draw up and interpret your own horoscope.

One thing about doing it yourself, which is an annoyance unless you are aware of it in advance: to calculate your horoscope properly you will need to know where the planets were in the sky when you were born, and you usually have to buy this data separately in a book called an ephemeris. The reason that astrology books don't have this data in them is that to include enough for everybody who is likely to buy the book would make the book as big as a phone directory, and look like a giant book of log tables, which is a bit off-putting. You can buy ephemerides (the plural) for any single year, such as the one of your birth. You can also buy omnibus versions for the whole century.

So, you will need two books, not one: an ephemeris, and a book to help you draw up and interpret your horoscope. It's much less annoying when you *know* you're going to need two books.

After that, there are lots of books on the more advanced techniques in the Astrology Handbook series, also from the Aquarian Press. Good though the books are, there is no substitute for being taught by an astrologer, and no substitute at all for practice. What we are trying to do here is provide a vocabulary of symbols taken from the sky so that you and your imagination can make sense of the world you live in; the essential element is your imagination, and you provide that.

Astrology works perfectly well at Sun sign level, and it works perfectly well at deeper levels as well; you can do it with what you want. I hope that, whatever you do with it, it is both instructive and satisfying to you—and fun, too.

SUNS AND LOVERS

The Astrology of Sexual Relationships

Penny Thornton. It doesn't seem to matter how experienced – or inexperienced – you are, when it comes to love and romance there just *isn't* a fool proof formula. . . but this book does its best to provide one! THE definitive astrological guide to sexual relationships, this book is based upon the accumulated wisdom, and observations of centuries of dedicated astrologists. Reveals:

- In-depth analysis of astrological types
- Male and female profiles for each star sign
- Zodiacal attitudes to intimate relationships
- Most compatible – and incompatible – partners

Each general star sign analysis is concluded with amazingly frank reflections, often based upon personal interviews, with many famous personalities including: Bob Champion; Suzi Quatro; Colin Wilson; Jeremy Irons; HRH The Princess Anne; HRH The Duke of York; Martin Shaw; Barbara Cartland; Twiggy and many more. Written in an easy-to-read style, and packed with illuminating and fascinating tit-bits, this book is compulsive reading for anyone likely to have *any sort* of encounter with the opposite sex!